NO MORE
LONE
RANGER
MOMS

*Women Helping Women
in the Practical
Everyday-ness of Life*

NO MORE LONE RANGER MOMS

DONNA PARTOW

BETHANY HOUSE PUBLISHERS
MINNEAPOLIS, MINNESOTA 55438

Published by Bethany House Publishers
A Ministry of Bethany Fellowship, Inc.
11300 Hampshire Avenue South
Minneapolis, Minnesota 55438

Printed in the United States of America.

Library of Congress Cataloging-in-Publication Data

Partow, Donna.
    No more lone ranger moms / Donna Partow.
       p. cm.
    Includes bibliographical references.

    1. Mothers—United States—Life skills guides. 2. Mothers—
Social networks—United States. 3. Babysitting cooperatives—
United States. I. Title.
HQ759.P29 1994
306.874'3—dc20   94–39002
ISBN 1–55661–531–0   CIP

This book is affectionately dedicated to my parents,

Jack and Olga Power.

I'm so glad you were both here to share this with me.

DONNA PARTOW is active in numerous mothers' support networks, including a weekly playgroup, a babysitting co-op, two home school support groups, a health food co-op, and a weekly ladies Bible study.

She's a regular speaker at women's retreats and conferences. She has also been a guest on numerous radio and television shows, including Focus on the Family, Parent Talk, Money Matters with Larry Burkett, and Moody Midday.

She and her family live in Arizona, where she home schools her daughter, Leah.

Special Thanks To

My Heavenly Father, who continues to lead me forward in the journey.

My precious daughter, Leah, who opened the door for me to "give up my career" and find a life beyond my wildest dreams.

Steve Laube, who rediscovered me when I was lost at sea.

Jerry and Mariette Holland—gentle mirror-holders and speech coaches *extraordinaire*.

Ann Meo, who restored my faith in friendship.

Gayle Pena, who brings beauty into every life she touches.

Randy Carlson and the gang at Today's Family Life. Thanks for welcoming me to Arizona and making me feel like part of the family.

Tess Nelson, my cheerleader, who will get a bigger kick out of this than anyone.

The women at the heart of my mothers' support network—each of whom has brought inspiration, encouragement and words of wisdom along the way: Gloria Chisholm, Cathy Guinan, Ann Klug, Diane Lilly, Dorrie McKee, Lynne Rienstra, Beth Riley, Cammy Scott, Helen Stellwag, Jan Whaley, and Anita Wingfield.

And to my husband, Cameron, who for fourteen years has sacrificially supported the choices I have made.

Foreword

AS THE HOST of the radio show *Parent Talk*, I deal with exhausted and discouraged Lone Ranger Moms every day. One typical phone call went something like this:

> I don't understand why God made me a mother. I mean, look at this place, I just cleaned it this morning and now I can't walk into one room of this house without having cereal crunch under my feet, sliding on spilled juice, or maiming myself on Legos. The laundry I folded earlier is scattered all over the house, and I just found my one-year-old eating my lipstick. My seven-year-old is home sick and has turned the living room into a fort. I don't know what I've gotten myself into. I'm an absolute failure. I just wasn't cut out to be a mother.

When I asked what, if any, support she had, there was deafening silence. After a moment, she made this unforgettable admission, "I'm afraid if the moms I see at Bible study knew how I felt, they'd think I wasn't a good Christian. I don't want to hear any lectures about how organized the Proverbs 31 woman was. I love my family, I just can't handle it all alone, but I don't know where to turn for help."

What this caller and thousands of other moms fail to

realize is that they don't have to go it alone. Motherhood is too important and too demanding to do alone without the support and encouragement of other moms. It is simply not designed for Lone Rangers. Strength can only come through community, not through a stiff upper lip. With this book, Donna Partow has provided a way out of the wilderness. She comes to the subject as a former Lone Ranger and gives the direction needed to dispel the pull-yourself-up-by-your-own-bootstraps mentality.

I heartily recommend both Donna and this book to you. Together you can blaze a trail through the desert of lonely motherhood to a renewed sense of community and a realization that together, with God's help, you can survive!

Randy Carlson
President of Today's Family Life
Host of *Parent Talk* radio

Contents

Part Three
The Reality

Part Four
The Wrap-Up

Introduction

I am living proof that God has a sense of humor. In a perfectly logical world, I would be the last person to write a book about overcoming the Lone Ranger syndrome. You see, I am the poster girl of the Lone Ranger movement. In fact, I've always been a loner. I guess I became one as a defensive ploy, because my seven older brothers and sisters had a penchant for trouble. By the time I came along, the world had rather limited expectations for me. Rejection greeted me at every turn, so I learned to keep to myself.

Over the years, I've taken great pride in my Lone Ranger status. Like Frank Sinatra, "I did it my way" and that suited me just fine. After all, the American ideal is symbolized by the Old West: rugged individuals blazing their own private trails across the wilderness. In 1992, I followed my soul-mate ancestors and trekked cross-country from New Jersey to Arizona. I left behind those seven siblings and everyone else I knew.

Along the way I discovered a surprising thing: *This motherhood trip wasn't designed for lone rangers*. It takes more than one woman against the world to raise a child in this increasingly complex and dangerous world. Even the pioneers sometimes circled the wagons. *Women need one another*. It's time to circle the wagons.

For some time I've perceived that women need to

hear that message. And I kept waiting for someone to send up the battle cry; someone to "send in the Cavalry." Years passed and the Cavalry never showed. All the while, a still small voice kept whispering in my ear, "Donna, *you* are the Cavalry. Get moving!" "But that's crazy," I countered. "How can I tell other women to reach out, to risk rejection? Who am I? I wake up terror-stricken in the middle of the night, sure that no one else on earth feels as vulnerable and alone as I do."

Yet, if there is one thing I've learned about God in my journey through life, it is this: He loves to choose the most unlikely job candidate. He's just the kind of God who would send the poster girl of the Lone Ranger movement to call an end to the standoff. Having experienced God's heavenly humor in the past, I began to see the power of His plan. So I prayed, "Lord, if you can set me free from the Lone Ranger syndrome, I promise to blaze the trail for others."

My turning point came a few days later when my husband sat me down for a heart-to-heart. (By the way, he didn't know anything about my little bargain with God.) "I know what's going on here," he said. "You may be fooling everyone else, but you're not fooling me. You've closed yourself off in your own little corner of the universe, with your books and your computer and your writing. You go out into the world, but you don't let anyone in. You think you're just playing it safe, but you're not really playing at all. And that's no way to live."

The next day, I picked up the phone and began networking with other mothers in my neighborhood. I was absolutely terrified, but I did it. And we all lived happily ever after, right? Not exactly. It hasn't been all fun and games for me, and it won't be for you, either. As you seek to break out of the Lone Ranger syndrome, you may get hurt. It's a very real possibility, and I want you to know that. When you let people into your life—when you allow yourself to need others and be needed by them—you are taking a huge risk. Remember this, though: without great risks, there can be no great rewards.

The greatest reward I have experienced is learning to accept who God made me to be. All my life, I've wished I could be like someone else—*anyone else*. I never came to grips with my weaknesses, so they continued to hold their grip on me. Through my women's support network, I've realized that God gives each of us humans a package deal: we get a set of strengths . . . and a set of weaknesses. Naturally, we'd prefer to pick and choose our characteristics. Then we'd be perfect, and we wouldn't need God or anyone else. It doesn't work that way.

For the first time in my life, I am beginning—just beginning—to actually accept the package God rolled together on the day He created me. And the women in my network have been instrumental in making that happen. I've found women who still love and respect me, even after seeing what my house looks like *when I'm not expecting company*. Women who have walked beside me *not* when I was Donna Partow best-selling author and motivational speaker, but when I was Donna Partow ordinary mom, battling the darkness of depression and fighting the emotional demons of my past. Women who've courageously held the mirror of truth before me and helped me confront those awful places that go bump in the night.

A rich journey awaits those of you who have the courage to join the wagon train. Sure, you'll travel over some treacherous trails and you might even get ambushed by a band of renegades. Just remember: it's your final destination that matters most.

The Strange State of Motherhood

The first time I noticed the puzzling state of modern motherhood, I was with my two-year-old daughter at a park. Eight preschool children played on swings, while seven young mothers (all with matching circles under their eyes) stood guard over their independent posts. "This is crazy," I thought. "At least ONE of us ought to go home and take a nap." And boy how I wished the napping mother was me!

Instead, we stood there quietly. Each enduring the exhausting rite of passage called "mother of preschoolers" like a hospital full of medical interns. No one lightens the load for anyone else; and no one asks for help for fear it might be interpreted as a sign of weakness. It's almost like a "macho woman" syndrome, complete with post-war stories and battle scars. I've even invented a term to describe mothers who believe they've got to go it alone; I call them Lone Ranger Moms. Right then, an idea was conceived. It continued to grow and is now being birthed on the pages of this book.

Think about it. It's just as easy to make two casseroles or two peanut butter and jelly sandwiches. It's as easy to entertain two children as one—in fact, it's often easier because they can entertain each other. (Well, usually.) I've found that inviting over a neighbor's child is an excellent way for me to . . . take a break! Yes, take a break. And everyone wins.

The children win because they get to play with someone other than boring old Mom. And they get to play with something other than their boring old toys (which they couldn't live without until you bought them, at which time they were immediately transformed into boring toys). The sending mom wins a reprieve. She can run errands, shop in peace, bathe, conduct business, read a book, or take a nap. The supervising mom wins because her child has something novel to do. She also has an opportunity to observe her child interacting with another child, which often leads to new insight. Of course, the biggest victory for the supervising mom is knowing that the sending mom will return the favor when the supervising mom needs to take a break! (If you follow the advice in this book and form a co-op, you'll find great joy in collecting co-op hour cards.)

Hosting children also helps mothers gain perspective. I remember feeling exasperated about Leah and clothes. She was three and a half at the time and would only wear dresses suitable for a senior prom. She changed ten times a day and immediately bundled up the clothes in her hamper. It made me crazy . . . until one day when her friend Alexandra came to play. She seemed just as much a slave to fashion as Leah.

Sure enough, when Alexandra's mother arrived, I discovered that she was experiencing the very same frustrations. We were both relieved to know our daughters were perfectly normal. We could have read about it in a book or talked about it at a women's Bible study, but reading and talking are not the same as firsthand experience.

In my Christmas letter last year, I wrote, "I want to issue a blanket apology to every parent I ever gave advice to. I had no clue." Motherhood is the one job no one can truly prepare you for; the only real training is the on-the-job variety. Unfortunately, we can't afford many mistakes. The stakes are just too high.

A battle is being waged and our children's future goes to the victor. We don't need statistics to prove it (although they are readily available in books like *Children at Risk* by Dr. James Dobson and Gary Bauer). We sense it. We feel the need to spread our wings of protection farther over our young.

As a woman who has decided to make motherhood a priority, you've made a great choice. Our society—especially the politicians, the media, and *some* so-called women's groups—may not applaud your efforts. But your job is the most important one in the world. Even if you have a career outside the home, the work you do in your home has far more eternal significance. Just as corporations are rediscovering the importance of teamwork, we need to apply those teamwork principles on the homefront. And we can.

Throughout this book, you'll find a step-by-step battle plan for uniting with other mothers in your church or community. I explain exactly how you can build and strengthen your own support network, based on my experience with numerous playgroups, co-ops, and home-school support groups. In researching this book, I've talked with women from all around the country.

I've included information explaining how to organize a formal mothers' support network—a group which might include one hundred women and encompass a broad range of activities. Suffice it to say, it's more work than one Lone Ranger mom can handle. Don't be intimidated! You don't have to form a large group, but if you want to, this book will show you how, step-by-step.

No More Lone Ranger Moms covers everything from "Finding Emotional and Practical Help" to "Building Your Own Support Network" and advice on how to handle the "Attack of the Killer Moms." I've included short, easy-to-read segments explaining the various activities you might organize (or convince someone else to organize).

If you just want to discover ways to form your own personal support network, or strengthen your existing women's fellowship, you'll find more than what you need on these pages. I've devoted a special section to "Ideas for Home Schooling Moms." Many mothers are opting to home school their children, to shield them from the insanity in many parts of the American public school system. Yet, home schooling mothers need to guard against isolation. In fact, many are already finding ways to join forces. In addition, there are numerous ideas on how to avoid the Lone Ranger Mom syndrome.

This book is a call for a new women's movement. Not for independence . . . but for interdependence. Not one born of anger toward men, but of love for one another. Not one to demand our rights, but to own up to our responsibility to help each other along this incredibly difficult journey called motherhood.

I'm just stubborn enough to believe I can launch a

whole new approach to mothering with this simple guidebook. (Actually, it's a very old approach; see Chapter 2.) My sister bought me a T-shirt that reads: "Warning: I am subject to sudden outbursts of enthusiasm." Indeed, I am. And I am very enthusiastic about the possibilities of moms helping moms in the practical, everyday-ness of life.

I know you are, too. That's why you are reading this book. I hope it serves as a helpful vehicle for you and the mothers around you. Happy trails!

How to Get the Most Out of This Book

You have this book because you feel a need to help other mothers—and to be helped by them. You are reading it because, deep within, you have a longing to connect, to share this wonderful and perplexing journey called motherhood.

Before you get started with Chapter 1, take a few moments to reflect on what you hope to achieve by reading this book. How will your life be better when you are finished? Set some specific goals. Perhaps you hope to strengthen your relationship with the mothers in your church or neighborhood. Perhaps there are just two or three other women you hope to connect with in a deeper way. Or maybe you have visions of launching a 300-member, statewide mothers' support network. It's up to you.

Although different readers will have different goals, one thing remains the same. If you really want to get the most out of this book, be sure to answer all of the questions and complete the exercises included in the "Take Time to Reflect" portion of each chapter. These items are not just an optional afterthought, but a vital part of the book. Taking time to apply what you've already learned is more important than rushing ahead to the next chapter.

If you are already part of an existing network, but

you see a need to strengthen your mutual commitment, you should encourage each of the members to obtain their own copy of *No More Lone Ranger Moms*. That way, you can work through the exercises together and learn as a group.

Whether you work through the book alone or in a group, it is my prayer that *No More Lone Ranger Moms* will strengthen you for the world's most important job— being a mom. And remember, you are not alone.

PART ONE

THE DILEMMA

Sage Advice from
Dr. James Dobson

IN HIS 1987 BOOK, *Love for a Lifetime* (Questar Publishers), Dr. James Dobson accurately describes the dilemma of young mothers today and offers some excellent advice to counteract its negative effect:

"I am especially concerned about the mother of small children who chooses to stay at home as a full-time homemaker. If she looks to her husband as a provider of all adult conversation and the satisfier of every emotional need, their marriage can quickly run aground. He will return home from work somewhat depleted and in need of 'tranquility.'

"Instead, he finds a woman who is continually starved for attention and support. When she sees in his eyes that he has nothing left to give, that is the beginning of sorrows. She either becomes depressed or angry (or both), and he has no idea how he can help her. I understand this feminine need and have attempted to articulate it to men.

"Nevertheless, a woman's total dependence on a man places too great a pressure on the marital relationship. It sometimes cracks under the strain.

"What can be done, then? A woman with a normal range of emotional needs cannot simply ignore them. They scream for fulfillment. Consequently, I have long recommended that women in this situation seek to supplement what their husbands can give by cultivating meaningful female relationships.

"Having girl friends with whom they can talk heart-to-heart, study the Scriptures, and share child-care techniques can be vital to mental health. Without this additional support, loneliness and low self-esteem can accumulate and begin to choke the marriage to death.

"This solution of feminine company seems so obvious that one might ask why it is even worthwhile to suggest. Unfortunately, it is not so easy to implement. A woman must often search for companionship today. We've witnessed a breakdown in relationships between women in recent years.

"A hundred years ago, wives and mothers did not have to seek female friendship. It was programmed into the culture. Women canned food together, washed clothes at the creek together, and cooperated in church charity together.

"When a baby was born, the new mother was visited by aunts, sisters, neighbors, and church women who came to help her diaper, feed, and care for the child. There was an automatic support system that surrounded women and made life easier. Its absence translates quickly into marital conflict and can lead to divorce.

"To the young wives who are reading these words, *I urge you to not let this scenario happen to you.* Invest some time in your female friends—even though you are busy. Resist the temptation to pull into the walls of your home and wait for your husband to be all things to you. Stay involved as a family in a church that meets your needs and preaches the Word.

"Remember that you are surrounded by many other women with similar feelings. Find them. Care for them. Give to them. And in the process, your own self-esteem will rise. Then when you are content, your marriage will flourish.

"It sounds simplistic, but that's the way we are made."

1
Home Alone

THE FIRST DAY I stayed at home alone, all day, I was absolutely terrified. In fact, I hid in my bedroom and kept perfectly still under the covers most of the day. (Remember when you were a little girl, and thought you could fool the bogeyman if you didn't breathe?) Don't get me wrong. We had a three-bedroom house in a safe, sleepy little suburb. The crime rate in our neighborhood was virtually nonexistent. Other than the occasional sound of my pacing feet (I had two weeks left until my due date), silence was the only sound. And boy did that frighten me!

Facing Loneliness Head-On

It was as if I'd awakened to discover myself transplanted to the middle of a ghost town. I was surrounded by row upon row of empty houses. Of perfectly manicured lawns that were glimpsed on the way out to work in the morning, not to be tread upon again until the end of the evening rush. The children were all packed off to daycare or preschool or some such place. And there I was, hunkered down, fighting the good fight as the last stay-at-home mom in America. Or so it seemed.

Gradually, I began to uncover signs of intelligent life in my suddenly small universe—the park, the pizza shop, the library. Yes, there were other moms who actually thought that being a mother was an important endeavor. We smiled knowingly, approvingly. Occasionally, we even ventured forth into polite conversation, but that's as far as it went.

Ah, this was not like the good old days. Not like when Mom and a host of comrades-carrying-bottles would swap stories, advice, and laughter over the back fence. Now we have five-foot-high solid concrete walls separating our homes. (Can you tell I live in Arizona?) It's not like the good old days when mothers didn't have to justify their decision to stay at home. We may debate whether or not our mother's generation really had it all figured out, but one thing is sure: we don't seem to.

The Search for Connectedness

Women still long for connectedness. We still want to belong to a group, an extended family. I believe that's the way God made us. Now, I could have conducted scientific studies into this matter. I could have interviewed world-famous psychologists and family experts. Instead, I'll just state my case and you can draw whatever conclusions you want. Fair enough?

Okay, here's my proof that women still search for connectedness. Soap operas. Soap operas? Yes. When I hear women talking about Luke and Laura as if they are part of their lives. . . When I hear children who think Luke and Laura *are* part of the family. . . When I see women buying magazines and tabloid newspapers devoted exclusively to soap opera characters. . . I know something is wrong.

If you've ever watched a soap, you know how addictive they often become. Have you ever thought about why? What technique do the writers use to draw in viewers on a consistent basis? They create an entire world, *another world*, if you will pardon the pun. The dialogue deals with the smallest details of everyday life, from the ordinary to the sublime. The characters become incredibly real—even though the scenarios they play out are often absurd. Not that I watch soaps, mind you, but I've heard on good authority that one actress on a popular soap has been married fifteen times.

Women who feel isolated from the real world find their connectedness with *another world*. The heroes and heroines are their friends, the villains become their enemies. All the emotion that should be poured into living real life is channeled into the vicarious life offered up on the tube.

Why Do Women Settle for So Much Less?

The question is: Why do some women settle for so much less? Why are millions content to experience life's joys and sorrows through someone else's make-believe life? I think it boils down to a sense of inadequacy. First, because our everyday lives lack enough excitement. There's nothing glamorous about changing diapers. Not many of us walk around the house in sequins. Not many of us have homes or husbands who look like the television ideal. Our world, when compared to others (both real and imagined), just doesn't measure up. Although I've never been addicted to soap operas, in many ways, I've settled for a life that is less than it could be.

Second, we sense that we ourselves are somehow "less than." Less important, less beautiful, less interesting, less. We long to connect, to be part of something better, but we're afraid we have nothing to offer. No one comes out and says this, of course, but it is "understood" that a woman who stays at home probably has a rather low IQ, very little education; she probably has no serious interests or talents and clearly has nothing of value to offer this society. Otherwise, she'd put her children in daycare and get back to work like the rest of the intelligent women. As one woman said, "When people ask me what I do, and I say, 'I'm staying home with the baby,' they say, 'Oh, what did you do before?' It's almost as if they expect me to try to vindicate myself."

How do I know this attitude prevails? I've heard it, time and again, from women who responded to my first book, *Homemade Business: A Woman's Step-by-Step Guide to Earning Money at Home* (Focus on the Family, June 1992). Millions of American women have bought into the messages being sent out by our culture—namely, that stay-at-home moms are somehow less important than everyone else. As a result, many stay-at-home moms have virtually no self-confidence left. They find it impossible to believe they have any talents or skills or that any of their ideas have merit.

I've seen this insecurity in women all over the country and in every age group. From women who've been at home for twenty years to women who've been at home for two months. I've heard it from women with college degrees and from women who should know better. What does all of this have to do with the Lone Ranger Mom syndrome? Plenty.

In our zeal to demonstrate that we are engaged in a worthy task—in fact, that we ourselves are worthy human beings, some mothers have gone to extremes. For such women, motherhood has become an all-consuming enterprise. She believes no one can care for her child like she can. True enough, but does that mean she should NEVER rely on a sitter? Never leave her child with a trusted friend? I recently met a woman who proudly announced that she hadn't been away from her children in three years. Ladies, this is not a good thing!

Although it's important to focus on your children, it's not healthy to become obsessive. It's not healthy for you and it's not healthy for them. When I worked as a youth leader, one of the toughest challenges teenagers faced was coping with a mother whose entire world revolved around them. Believe me, the weight of an overzealous mom's unrealistic expectations is a heavy load to bear.

The Perils of "Time Drift"

In order to be the best mother you can be, you need a life beyond your role as mother. But how will you ever find time to pursue other interests if you insist on being a Lone Ranger mom? You won't! Instead, your days will drift endlessly, one day into the next. It's called "time drift."

What do I mean by time drift and why should you be concerned about it? Let me give you an example. Shortly before Easter, I took my daughter, Leah, to the mall for her holiday picture. Her appointment was scheduled for 10:00 A.M. and I decided to run a bunch of errands when we were finished. We went here and there, picked up this and that. Finally, in our famished state, we stopped by the mall's Food Court to grab a bite to eat. I looked at my watch and gasped out loud: it was 3:00 o'clock.

The woman next to me, with a preschooler by her side, looked at me sympathetically. "Hard to believe, isn't it?" she marveled. We then had one of those "Thank God, it's not just me" conversations. "Every night, my husband walks in the door and says 'What did you do all day?' " she noted. "I always tell him the same thing. 'I have no idea what I did all day, but I do know I never sat down.' "

I knew exactly what she meant, because my husband and I have the same conversation all the time. The days seem to drift away in an endless blur of cooking and eating, shopping and errands, puzzles and stories, coloring and painting, cleaning and making a mess, loading and unloading the dishwasher. The washing machine virtually cries out for the next batch of dirty-again clothes. I'm constantly working, but nothing is ever DONE. And the days drift on and on. A week has passed, a month has passed, and my daughter just had her fourth birthday. It's "time drift" and unless you find a place to anchor yourself, you're identity will drift away just as surely, just as quietly.

I know, because I've felt it happening to me. Just this morning, I sat on the couch, wrapped safely in my husband's arms and cried, "How can it be April? How can this house be a mess again? Where did the last year go?" For the first time, my husband really seemed to understand. Several weeks ago, I was hospitalized with pneumonia. The doctors said the recovery would probably take eight weeks and I was put on bed rest. Of course, I laughed. We all know there's no such thing as rest for Mom.

My husband has tried hard to pick up the slack, since walking from one room to the next leaves me exhausted and gasping for breath. He remarked, "I just unloaded this dishwasher and now it's full again." He was truly astounded. "No kidding," I said. "Now remember, for the past twelve years, I didn't HAVE a dishwasher." He also discovered the laundry. "It's just too hard," he said, after tossing three loads in. He didn't even attempt folding.

How Did Mom Do It?

Even in the midst of this, I can hear my mother's voice in the back of my mind, *I didn't have a dishwasher and I had eight kids. And I not only folded, I hung the laundry out to dry on clotheslines.* How DID she do it? I wonder. Why am I struggling so hard just to keep up with one child? A sense of inadequacy overwhelms me. And I begin to wonder: am I the only mother in the world who feels this way? Am I the only one who can't seem to get it together? This motherhood business isn't exactly rocket science, why can't I do it? I must be a complete failure.

Finding Support

As **Dr. Dobson** noted, young mothers today rarely have the ready-made support system offered by nearby family members. The kind of support that our mothers and grandmothers could take for granted. That's why it is so important for you to take the initiative to join an organization like MOPS (Mothers of Preschoolers) or a similar mothers' group. Take advantage of the regularly scheduled meetings as a place to begin building deeper relationships. Of course, you can't build a vital support network if all you do is "attend and go home." That's why meeting new people is called net*working* not net-*sitting* or net-*eating*. It's hard work to reach out and ask for the support you need. It's harder still to *offer help*.

Instead of sitting back and soaking in, get actively involved. Offer to bring refreshments or to help out by teaching a craft. Invite some of the women to your home during the week, or perhaps invite several women and their husbands over for a Saturday afternoon barbecue. Chances are the other mothers in the group struggle with the exact same issues you face. Don't wait for someone to reach out to you, take the initiative and set the pace.

"Just going to my first MOPS was a big step for me," says Suzan Standfast of Tempe, Arizona. Suzan says the group has helped her deal with loneliness while building her leadership skills. "I dropped out of work and school when I became a mom. I don't have homework, I don't have colleagues. My family is several hundred miles away, and my husband works from three in the afternoon to midnight. I hardly ever see him. I was always a loner, but I never felt lonely until I became a mom."

Suzan says MOPS is her "lifeline." She explains, "It's just like business networking. We can connect with people we otherwise wouldn't have access to. We've also learned to pool our resources and creativity, even outside our regular meetings. Last summer, one lady from our group organized field trips for the kids. We went to the dairy, to local parks, and other activities. She even arranged a special discount rate at Discovery Zone—a great place to let the kids burn off excess energy. It wasn't that much more effort for her to plan for everyone. In fact, she enjoyed doing it and felt great about using her talents. And, of course, it made everyone else's job that much easier. All we had to do was show up."

Elisa Morgan, President of **MOPS** International, describes the meetings as "a haven for soothing frazzled nerves and forming lifelong friendships." The mothers listen to teaching from an experienced mother who shares biblical truths and practical ways to fulfill the varied roles of mother, wife, and woman. Next, the women break into discussion groups—an encouraging, accepting atmosphere where they can express their feelings on motherhood and marriage.

In addition, women have an opportunity to complete a craft project—something they probably wouldn't have the time or energy to do at home. Best of all, moms get to do all this without little ones climbing all over them! That's because the children participate in their own special program, called **MOPPETS**. There are now about 850 **MOPS** groups. If you'd like to join one or start a **MOPS** program in your area, contact them at:

MOPS International, Inc.
1311 S. Clarkson
Denver, CO 80210
(303) 733–5353

Perhaps the most important lesson your support network will teach you is this: no mother is perfect. Relax and do your best. Learn from one another, in both victory and defeat. It is my hope and prayer that this book will become a vital tool to help members of **MOPS** and similar groups to build and strengthen one another.

Take Time for Reflection

1. List three moms you see on a regular basis but have never really gotten to know. If you don't even know her name, write "woman at park." For each of the women, list several ways you can begin to reach out to them in friendship:

NAME   HOW I WILL REACH OUT

_____   _____

                              _____

                              _____

_____   _____

                              _____

                              _____

_____   _____

                              _____

                              _____

2. If you watch soap operas, take a few moments to reflect on why you do so. Is it possible that you are finding a false sense of connectedness through your involvement with the TV characters? Look inside yourself for answers.

_____

_____

_____

_____

3. Do you ever feel "less than" because you are a stay-at-home mom? Pretend you are your boss and complete the following Job Performance Evaluation. Circle the appropriate job rating for each item:*

ASSIGNMENT	RATING			
Feed the family	Fabulous	Great	Good	Uh-oh
Change the baby	Fabulous	Great	Good	Uh-oh
Rock & burp baby	Fabulous	Great	Good	Uh-oh
Bathe the kids	Fabulous	Great	Good	Uh-oh
Answer ALL questions	Fabulous	Great	Good	Uh-oh
Keep floors clean	Fabulous	Great	Good	Uh-oh
Give "talking to's"	Fabulous	Great	Good	Uh-oh
Phone receptionist	Fabulous	Great	Good	Uh-oh
Hygienist	Fabulous	Great	Good	Uh-oh
Babysitting supervisor	Fabulous	Great	Good	Uh-oh
Teacher	Fabulous	Great	Good	Uh-oh
Homework helper	Fabulous	Great	Good	Uh-oh
TV Censor	Fabulous	Great	Good	Uh-oh
Party planner	Fabulous	Great	Good	Uh-oh
Out-loud book reader	Fabulous	Great	Good	Uh-oh
Short-order cook	Fabulous	Great	Good	Uh-oh
Repairwoman	Fabulous	Great	Good	Uh-oh
On-site exterminator	Fabulous	Great	Good	Uh-oh
Resident historian	Fabulous	Great	Good	Uh-oh
Human encyclopedia	Fabulous	Great	Good	Uh-oh
Expert food preserver	Fabulous	Great	Good	Uh-oh
Social secretary	Fabulous	Great	Good	Uh-oh
Librarian	Fabulous	Great	Good	Uh-oh
Chief correspondent	Fabulous	Great	Good	Uh-oh
Ironer of wrinkles	Fabulous	Great	Good	Uh-oh
Tax preparer (!?!)	Fabulous	Great	Good	Uh-oh
Spiritual guide	Fabulous	Great	Good	Uh-oh
Pray-er	Fabulous	Great	Good	Uh-oh
Fitness expert	Fabulous	Great	Good	Uh-oh

*Adapted from *Mom, You're Incredible* by Linda Weber (Focus on the Family, 1994).

Bargain finder	Fabulous	Great	Good	Uh-oh
Nutritionist	Fabulous	Great	Good	Uh-oh
Car waxer	Fabulous	Great	Good	Uh-oh
Oven cleaner	Fabulous	Great	Good	Uh-oh
Interior decorator	Fabulous	Great	Good	Uh-oh
EMT	Fabulous	Great	Good	Uh-oh
Postmaster	Fabulous	Great	Good	Uh-oh
Hair stylist	Fabulous	Great	Good	Uh-oh
Banker	Fabulous	Great	Good	Uh-oh
Volunteer	Fabulous	Great	Good	Uh-oh
Hugger	Fabulous	Great	Good	Uh-oh
Boo-boo kisser	Fabulous	Great	Good	Uh-oh
Much more	Fabulous	Great	Good	Uh-oh

4. Now, write yourself a memo of commendation (again posing as your own boss) congratulating yourself on the great job you're doing as a mother:

DATE: _____

FROM: The Chief Honcho-VIP-Always Right Boss

TO: _____

RE: Outstanding Job Performance

_____

_____

_____

_____

_____

_____

_____

_____

_____

_____

5. Hopefully, those two exercises boosted your confidence in yourself as a capable, hard-working person. List some other ways you can boost your confidence level:

_____

_____

_____

6. When was the last time you spent more than three hours away from your children?_____
If you answered more than six months ago, it's time to get away. Assuming your children are weaned, make plans *right now* to do just that. Complete the following planning exercise:

   I, _____ (name), have been guilty of over-mothering. There are other people who can and will take care of my children so that I can have some time to get re-invigorated for the challenging task of mothering.
   Therefore, I plan to go to _____ (where) on _____(date) from _____o'clock to _____o'clock. While I am there, I plan to enjoy activities such as _____,
_____, _____,
_____, and _____. I can ask any one of the following people to watch my child(ren) while I enjoy three hours on my own:
_____, or _____, or _____.
I will contact these people today to make the necessary arrangements. And while I am gone, I won't even call to check on how things are going. (Well, maybe just once.)

7. When is the last time you and your spouse went away overnight, alone together?_____
If you answered more than a year ago, it's time to get away. Assuming your children are weaned, make plans *right now* to do just that. It's time to complete another planning exercise:

   We, _____(husband) and _____

(wife), recognize that the greatest gift we can give our children is our love for each other as husband and wife. It may be difficult, but we will find a trusted friend or relative who will take care of our children so we can have some time to focus on our marriage.

Therefore, we plan to go to _____ (where) from _____ (date/time) until _____ (date/time). We can ask the following people to watch our children while we enjoy a weekend alone: _____, or _____, or _____. We will contact these people today to make the necessary arrangements. And while we are gone, we'll try not to call home more than five times a day.

Now, don't you feel better already?!

8. Read the following essay on "A Wal-Mart Kind of Day" and have a good laugh. If you think it might help, try Wal-Marting yourself.

A Wal-Mart Kind of Day
by Stacey C. York

IT HAS BEEN ONE of those days when I wonder where my patience went. From the time I started mopping the kitchen floor first thing this morning (while trying to keep peace among two children and a kitten) I knew it was going to be a Wal-Mart kind of day.

My neighborhood friends and I developed the term "Wal-Marting" during our conversation one afternoon. I find that my troubles seem less significant when I'm outside—even more so when I'm talking to another mother at home about common concerns.

Wal-Marting goes something like this: My day has gotten progressively worse. Any slight deviation from routine sets off my temper. My children seem particularly fussy. We run out of juice midday. The kitten keeps using the couch as a scratching post. Two unexpected bills come in the mail and I get four phone calls during naptime. I can hardly wait for my husband to get home from work. As he walks through the door and asks me how my day has been, I explain that I am in need of some alone time. He says he'll see me later. I hop into the car and head to Wal-Mart.

It feels good to be out without a diaper bag. As I park the car, I begin a mental shopping list. An immediate sense of relief hits me as I grab a cart. I am there to shop without anyone running off or begging for toys. I stop at the food counter for a diet Coke. As I head to the baby department, my shoulders return to the normal position on my body rather than the position they have been occupying next to my ears all afternoon! I get a sense of comfortable familiarity as I walk past the baby food, teething toys, and socks.

When my cart is loaded, I browse. We do not really need anything else but a prescription, and in this time of careful budgeting, we are trying not to buy impulsively. Just the same, I pick up some batteries, scotch tape, and weed killer. Next I stroll over to the pharmacy. As I sit on the bench waiting for the prescription, I am amazingly relaxed. I could be in a quiet meadow (well, almost) as I watch shoppers walk by. A clerk is stocking shelves. Other parents are frantically chasing children and apologizing for accidental spills and mishaps, but I am calm. Even waiting an extra five or ten minutes for my medication doesn't upset me. I am enjoying the shopping center solitude.

As I head for the check-out counter, I have an enormous sense of accomplishment. I have gotten the needed items and managed to relax and restore my patience. I am ready to go home and begin the bedtime routine.

Had someone told me five years ago, when my first priority was building a career, that the highlight of my week would become, on occasion, Wal-Marting, I would have replied, "Never in my lifetime!" Now I have difficulty imagining things any other way.

Reprinted with permission from *Welcome Home*, March 1993.

2
Finding Emotional and Practical Support

IN HER EXCELLENT BOOK *The Stay-at-Home Mom* (Harvest House, 1991), Donna Otto shares a wonderful anecdote that gave her insight into how Native American mothers once supported one another. It beautifully and simply illustrates the main concept behind *No More Lone Ranger Moms*:

> I was recently camping with my husband in a park in California. While on a hike we came upon a huge, flat outcropping of rock about 40 feet wide. Worn into the top of the rock was a series of equal-sized indentations where Indian women ground corn for hundreds of years. It was a job each woman had to do, and it could have been done alone. But they gathered on the rock to enjoy each other's presence as they worked. It must have made the work of making cornmeal much more enjoyable. They came together as sisters, understanding the value of support while doing a task together. (p. 163)

Grandma's Playing Tennis

Native American women weren't the only ones who provided practical support to one another. Things were much different, even during our parents' generation. "When I was young," notes Ann Meo, one of the key women in my support network, "all the mothers on the block stayed home. My cousins, aunts, and grandparents lived around the corner. You don't have that anymore. Stay-at-home moms have to really search for a support network." But where can we turn? A natural choice seems to be turning to older women for help. However, in my interviews with hundreds of women throughout the country, I've discovered that inter-generational support (from family or non-family members) is extremely rare in modern America.

"Only five percent of American children see a grandparent regularly, a much lower level than in the past," notes David Hamburg, writing in *Today's Children*. "We can no longer take for granted the supportive systems that were built into human experience over [thousands] of years."

One young mother summed up the view of many when she said, "Older women took their turn. Now they get to play tennis and golf and take cruises. Now they get to relax and we get to suffer." She harbored no bitterness. She simply accepted that this is the way motherhood passed from one generation to the next. Let's remember: it was not always so.

Every Woman for Herself

If we can't turn to previous generations for help, as mothers have done for thousands of years, can we rely on our peers? Historically, American women married and had children in their late teens and early twenties. Girls who went to elementary and high school together, entered marriage and child-rearing at the same time and in the same neighborhood. The bonds of friendship and mutual trust were already established.

Contrast that with the 1990s, when women are giving birth to children—sometimes their first—in their thirties and forties. Many of their peers are well beyond the preschool parenting age. Meanwhile, the women around them "in the same boat" may be much younger and share very little common experience. The result? Women drift apart, as those who marry and parent early live a totally different lifestyle from the full-time, single career woman. The ties of friendship become increasingly difficult to maintain.

Margaret Rosen, in her article "All Alone: The New Loneliness of American Women," observes that "friends are the first things women cut when balancing demands." Many women are just too tired. Still others expect their husband to be their best friend and to fill all their needs—a very unrealistic expectation (*Ladies Home Journal*, April 1991, p. 140).

Egesangio—An Equally Shared Thing

Can women really rely on one another for help in the practicalities of everyday life? Absolutely. In fact, support networks are extremely common in many other parts of the world. Lyn Dobrin of Westbury, New York, recalls her experience as a Peace Corps volunteer in Kisii, western Kenya. She lived among the people there from 1965 to 1967. "My job was to help the farmers understand the principles of running a cooperative. It was an easy concept to teach throughout Africa and in Kisii, where work was divided quite rigidly, and cooperative structures already existed throughout the culture. Most of the agricultural work was performed by the women: hoeing, sowing, weeding, and harvesting. Women were also responsible for cooking, collecting firewood, and grinding grain.

"In Kisii, the women in neighboring homesteads form cooperative groups to accomplish their agricultural chores. These types of groups are called *egesangio* (pronounced egg-a-sang-io), which means an equally shared thing. The egesangio groups move from homestead to homestead, helping each other to perform chores. One day, they might be at one woman's house and the next at another. They continue working until all women have received an equal share of work from the egesangio.

"While in Kisii, I helped organize a special project using the egesangio. The women decided they would each like to have a special outdoor table at which they could wash clothes, dishes, or small children. Such tasks were usually performed at the river or bent over a basin on the ground. With the help of an extension worker from the local Department of Community Development, we designed a waist-high wooden wash table. We went to the first woman's house where we dug a ditch two feet deep by four feet by three feet wide. In the four corners, we placed uprights that reached a height of approximately four feet and filled in the hole with large stones for drainage. The uprights formed the four legs of the table; they were joined together by four horizontal pieces of wood to create the foundation for the top of the table. The rest of the table consisted of additional pieces of wood hammered into place across the top frame. In subsequent days, the women went to each other's homes, building the tables."

Would It Work Here and Now?

Okay, you're thinking: that kind of cooperation was great for mothers in early America. And it's just wonderful for those women in Kenya. But can American mothers today make it work, here and now? Again, the answer is a resounding yes. You're about to meet dozens of mothers, from all parts of the country, who are sharing the tasks of motherhood and helping one another in creative and powerful ways.

Practical Help, American-Style

During the summer of 1982, I worked as a nanny/ housekeeper for a seminary professor and his wife, Dave and Nan Powlison, in suburban Philadelphia. They lived in a large house that had been converted into a twin home. Nan and her neighbor, Linda Blakeman, were among the pioneers of the modern co-op movement, although they had a rather informal approach. "Our husbands were both leaders in the local church, so that kept us very busy. Because our homes were actually attached, it was easy for us to trade off babysitting or pick up something for each other when we went to the store," recalls Linda.

Nan and Linda also helped share the cooking load. Between the two families, they had eight mouths to feed three times a day. "One night I would cook, the next night Nan would make a double casserole. We didn't have a system per se, but we were always looking for ways to lighten each other's load."

Nan and Linda were also pioneers of the playgroup movement. At that time, preschools were not as common as they are today and the word *playgroup* hadn't been invented. Linda recalls, "We just made it up as we went along. Of course, it would have been much easier if we had a handbook to guide the way. All we knew is that many of our friends had children around the same age. We wanted to let our kids play together and we knew we needed a break."

Linda organized five mothers into a playgroup. "Once a week, all of the children would gather at one of the mothers' homes for several hours one morning. It was her responsibility to invent something fun for the kids to do. Whether it was making teepees in the backyard, finger painting, or walking to a nearby park. The rest of us could go shopping, catch up on housework, take a bath, or whatever. It worked great for all of us," recalls Linda.

Sometimes You Just Need To Talk

Although Linda is a very practical person, there came a time in her life when all she wanted was someone to talk to. "We were having problems with our son, Jeff, who had been diagnosed with Attention Deficit Disorder (ADD). I was struggling as a mother because Jeff didn't fit the mold and I wasn't comfortable with it. The trouble with Jeff put a wall between me and my husband. Neither of us could figure out 'the right way' to handle him. I felt very alone and desperately needed someone to talk to. We decided to put Jeff in counseling and one week I asked his counselor if I should make an appointment for myself. All I really needed was someone to talk to, but I felt guilty asking my very busy friends to just sit and listen to me." Some time later, Linda went on a woman's retreat and decided to speak up. In exasperation, she exclaimed, "This is sick. I have to pay for a friend. Is that what our culture has come to?" To her amazement, every one of the women in the room—without exception—said, "Linda, I feel the same way."

That was three years ago. Since then, four women have been getting together every Wednesday night at 8:30 P.M. "Our mission is simply to support one another. To just be friends. We pray. We talk about issues. It's not formal, but it's understood that everyone gets a turn to talk about her concerns."

Linda reports that since the group formed, each of the women has had "major, major issues come up" and they've worked through it together. "What's incredible to me is that I've known two of these women for fifteen years and I never really knew them. Our relationships were so superficial. Now our goal is to get beyond shallow friendship and talk about real issues.

"I have too many surface relationships," says Linda. "People today are afraid to deal with real problems. We don't want to tell anyone that we're struggling or that we're depressed. What I was looking for, and what I found, were real, committed relationships. Along the way, we've discovered that our battles are really all the same. It all boils down to this: "Is God good and does He care? We're all grappling with those two key questions."

Twice a year, the women go away for a weekend together and leave the kids at home with Dad. Occasionally, the women plan special dinners for all the husbands. Linda's advice to a young woman who is feeling lonely is, "You've got to express your need to other people. You may be very surprised to find that others feel the same way. Don't grin and bear it. That's not helping anything. It's okay to say 'I needed you, where were you?' Say it in love, but speak up."

Today, Linda's children are older (Jeff, 14; Ann, 12; and John, 10) and she's too smart to play the macho-woman game. "I'm done playing the game where we say everything is under control. 'I've got it all together.' I don't have it all together, and that's okay. I think the pre-school years would have been easier to get through if I'd been more willing to admit that a long time ago."

Sometimes Talk Isn't Enough

Cynthia Fantasia walked through a dark valley . . . a place where talk just wasn't enough. Her husband, a successful executive, suddenly lost his job. For the next eighteen months, he endured the pain and frustration of unemployment. Cynthia endured it, too. Yet, as the Director of Women's Ministries for a large church in New England, Cynthia often felt pressured to put up a good front. A lot of people asked Cynthia how she was doing; a lot of people were willing to talk superficially about "how hard it must be." People who actually *did something* to help were much harder to find.

Cynthia was having a particularly bad day when a woman rushing by her in the church parking lot said off-handedly, "Oh, Cynthia, I'm praying for you." Cynthia recalls the moment well. "Suddenly I just couldn't take it anymore. Months of frustration swept over me and something just snapped. And I thought, 'Is that all she can do? Couldn't she at least call me?'"

As the Bible says, "Suppose a brother or sister is without clothes and daily food. If one of you says to him, 'Go, I wish you well; keep warm and well fed,' but does nothing about his physical needs, what good is it?" (James 2:15–16). Fortunately, there were a handful of women who went beyond talk to offer Cynthia practical help. One such woman, Margaret, was a pastor's wife from a small nearby church. Cynthia knew the family had very little money. Yet, one day this woman showed up on Cynthia's doorstep with enough fresh-picked corn to last several months.

"I was stunned. How could she possibly afford to bring us such a gift? When I asked where she got it, she refused to tell me. It wasn't until many months later that my friend finally told me the truth. She lived next to a large farm, and the farmer let her glean the field. This woman had spent an entire day working in a cornfield, under intense summer heat, gathering up corn the harvesters had missed. She and her husband worked for hours that evening to husk the corn, strip it off the cob, cook it, and store it in meal-sized bags. The really wonderful part was, every time I opened the freezer, I knew someone cared about me."

What an incredible contrast. One woman talked; another sacrificed and toiled to provide practical help to a friend. Which kind of woman are you? When you see someone in need, do you take action? So often, we feel that since we can't solve the problem entirely, we shouldn't bother to do anything. This humble pastor's wife could not offer an executive position to Cynthia's husband. She had no high-powered contacts, no friends in high places. But she could glean corn. So that's what she did.

Don't despise small things. They can mean so very

much. Last year, my husband was unemployed for nearly ten months. During that time, I wrote an article, "Out of Work: One Family's Journey" for *Focus on the Family*, a Christian magazine read by some 2.5 million people. Within days, our phone began ringing off the hook. From six o'clock in the morning until eleven o'clock at night, hundreds of calls poured in from all over the United States and Canada.

However, they were not calling to offer us practical help. Instead, they called with their own agendas. Most of the callers wanted us to buy starter kits to become distributors for various multi-level marketing companies. There are certainly many companies that offer good opportunities to make extra money at home. My point is simply this: where was the practical concern that one human being should have for another?

I'm happy to report that one sixteen-year-old girl from Michigan sent an anonymous letter to my daughter, Leah. She enclosed a pack of gift certificates for McDonald's. I had mentioned in the article how much Leah loved Happy Meals, but we had not been able to buy them lately. You would not believe how much joy those certificates brought to Leah. Or how many times, when I felt such disappointment in other people, her gesture of kindness kept my faith alive.

Cynthia shares that similarly small acts of kindness were enough to keep her going, as well. "One woman bought me a Day-Timer for the New Year. It was a really special gift, because it was her way of acknowledging that my time still mattered. That I still had 'important' things to do, even if my husband wasn't rushing off to an 'important' job."

It's amazing how the simple things can bother you when you're going through a financial crisis like unemployment. Cynthia recalls, "This sounds stupid, but what bothered me the most was being very aware that my clothes were fading. Now, I love bright colors. If I know a woman is struggling financially, I give her a bright-colored scarf. It doesn't cost me that much and when she puts it on, suddenly her old and worn outfits look new. A small gesture like that can bring so much joy. And the point is, it's not hard to do. It's just a matter of taking the time and caring enough to show your concern."

Another special gift is laughter and fun. "We had a friend who would bake a couple dozen chocolate chip cookies for us every once in a while," says Cynthia. "It didn't cost her much, but it was such a treat for our family. Knowing that she took the time to bake especially for us was very special."

Of course, sometimes large acts of kindness are in order. And if you can afford to help in a big way, be willing. Cynthia recalls one such event. "During my lowest time, one friend sat down in my office and asked me how I was doing. After I gave her the official response, she got up and shut the door and said, 'This is me. What's really happening?' What was really happening is that my son would soon have to drop out of college. We were flat out of money. That's when she made an incredible promise: 'Your son will not have to come home. I will pay his way.'

"I told her in tears and shame, I found it too hard to trust and believe anymore. She said. 'I know. Let me trust and believe for you.' As I look back, what a tremendous gift she gave me. No lectures, no finger-pointing, just understanding. Thanks to her, I don't have the bad memory of walking away from God. Instead, a dear friend carried me through."

Unfortunately, many women have lost the art of responding on the spur of the moment with small gestures that show we care. We need to reawaken that within ourselves. If you feel like doing something for another woman, even if it seems insignificant, just do it. How often do you say to a friend, "I thought of you the other day." Well, show them. Act on the impulse. Drop them a note. Pick up the phone. Buy them a $2.00 gift at the store. Make an extra dozen cookies or an extra casserole. It's easy to do and means so much.

A great resource for demonstrating small gestures of concern is the *Current* catalog. It is filled with greeting cards and note cards at very affordable prices. You'll also find stickers, rubber stamps, writing tablets, mailing labels, wrapping paper, ribbons, bows, and a lot more. Caring doesn't have to cost a fortune, and if you order from a catalog like *Current*, you don't even have to run to the store. You can just reach in your "caring drawer" or "caring file" and quickly act on your impulse of concern.

To obtain a free catalog, call or write:

Current
The Current Building
Colorado Springs, CO 80941
1–800–525–7170

We can recover the lost art of caring . . . and it can begin with you.

Take Time for Reflection

1. Call your mother and ask her to describe what her life was like when she was in your shoes. Did she associate with many other mothers? What types of things did they do together? How did they help each other? If it's not possible to talk with your mother, seek out another woman from her generation. Make a note of any insights she shares with you:

_____

_____

_____

_____

2. Do you know anyone who is from or has lived in a foreign country? Ask them to tell you about motherhood in their part of the world. Specifically, ask how women in their countries provide practical help to one another. Note any insights you gain:

_____

_____

_____

_____

_____

3. Do you have women in your life you can *really* talk to? If so, take a minute right now to send each of them a note card, expressing your appreciation for their genuine friendship. If

you don't have any women in your life you can really talk to, you need to find someone.

4. Make a list of women you would like to develop a deep relationship with. Do not list more than three names. Call at least one of them right now and arrange to get together over coffee. Talk about the realities of mothering. Get beyond the superficial to really talk about the victories and defeats you've faced recently.

_____

_____

_____

5. Can you think of a time when you needed someone to talk to, and no one was there for you? Recall how that felt. Jot down your thoughts.

_____

_____

_____

6. Can you think of a time when you needed a friend to do *more than talk*; a time when what you really needed was practical help? Was someone there to help you? If so, take time to express your appreciation to her. If not, reflect upon how you felt. Jot down your thoughts.

_____

_____

_____

7. Reflecting upon the story about the wife whose husband was unemployed, which kind of a friend are you? Are you the kind who would rush by in the church parking lot with a casual greeting? Or are you the kind who would glean corn?

Which kind of friend do you want to be? Be honest with yourself.

_____

_____

_____

_____

8. When was the last time you "gleaned corn" for a friend? That is to say, when was the last time you sacrificed your time and energy in order to provide practical help to a friend? How did you feel about yourself? Describe:

_____

_____

_____

_____

9. No doubt there are many women around you who are in need of help right now. Make a list of names and needs—then take action to show that you have managed to recover the lost art of small gestures.

NAME   NEED

_____   _____

_____   _____

_____   _____

_____   _____

_____   _____

10. Make a list of clubs and organizations you are involved in now that could possibly grow from talk-based

to practical-help-based groups. Plan to discuss the ideas you've read in this book with the group's leader. (Better yet, buy her a copy!)

ORGANIZATION   LEADER

_____   _____

_____   _____

_____   _____

11. Make a list of women you know (ideally women who live within two miles of your home) who might be interested in working together to provide mutual support:

_____

_____

_____

_____

_____

_____

3
What's the Holdup?

THIS CARING AND SHARING sounds great, doesn't it? Which brings us to the key question: Why don't we bother? What's the holdup? When we really think about it, it IS just as easy to make two casseroles. It IS just as easy to entertain two children. It IS easy to pick up an extra gallon of milk. It IS easy to buy a small gift. Why don't we? And why don't we just drop by a friend's house? Why do we feel like we need an agenda? Let's take a quick look at some of the reasons:

Mobility

Americans don't stay in one place for very long. Although the statistics vary from state to state, the average American family moves once every four years. It's hard to establish trusting relationships when you're on the move. It's especially hard when you feel like you're just passing time until your family is transferred to the next city.

It also can be difficult to establish common ground with women who grew up in distant parts of the country, with different values and customs. Once upon a time, it was the "odd fellow" who kept to herself and didn't know her neighbors well. Today it's the odd fellow who tries to strike up a conversation; we're immediately suspicious of her motives.

Time Constraints

It has become the battle cry of our society: "Who has time?" And the answer seems to be, "No one." Anyone can talk, that's easy to do. But it takes time to show you care in practical ways. Unfortunately, time is something most of us feel we don't have enough of. And when we get a spare moment, we need the time for ourselves. The truth is, we'd probably find ourselves MORE refreshed if we invested our time in caring for others—rather than soaking in a hot bathtub.

That's not to say that soaking in a hot bathtub is not just what the doctor ordered on some occasions. Yes, we need to attend to ourselves. But most of us have gone too far. Dr. Tony Campolo says it best in his book *20 Hot Potatoes Christians Are Afraid to Touch* (Word, 1988):

> Doing good and serving others are [a great way] out of the doldrums. . . . The missionary organization which I helped to establish, the Evangelical Association for the Promotion of Education, has an outreach program among urban children who are having problems with their schoolwork. In order to help these children, our organization enlists people to tutor them and to help them with their homework.
>
> As we did our initial recruiting, we were able to find a half-dozen very well educated women who were free and willing to help us in our efforts. Two of them were in psychotherapy because their negative feelings about themselves were so severe. But these two women were in for a surprising transformation. As they helped troubled inner-city children, they themselves found help. In serving the children, they began to sense their own worth. Doing something important for others made them feel that they

were important. One of the women . . . acknowledged that working with the kids had done more
good for her than had her therapist.

I can never understand why people who are
down on themselves do not grasp how easy it is to
re-define their worth through meaningful service to
others. . . . I know that if those who are depressed
would forget themselves and lose themselves in
other people who need them, they would realize a
great sense of self-worth. (pp. 28–29)

The only way to break free from the chains that iso-
late us is to invest our time in the lives of others. Time
is our most precious possession. And like any other investment, the amount of reward we can hope to attain
is directly related to the amount of risk we are willing
to assume. In order to save time and make your life easier in the long run, you have to invest your time wisely
right now. That will mean taking risks. It will also mean
you'll have to endure some inconvenience in the short
run in order to reap the rewards of friendship and support in the long run.

Personal Insecurity

We are so quick to assume, "Oh, she probably doesn't
like me. She probably wouldn't want to spend time with
me." We don't reach out because we fear rejection. And
it becomes a vicious cycle: we don't reach out, so no one
reaches out to us, so we feel rejected, so we don't reach
out. Someone has to end the cycle of isolation. Will it be
you?

Yes, there is always the risk that the other person will
reject you. But that's just part of life. I often play a little
joke on my audiences when I speak at various conferences. Here's what I tell them: "Research indicates that
50% of the people you meet will like you and 50% won't.
Now turn to your right. That person likes you. Feels

good, doesn't it? Now turn to your left. Uh-oh! According-
ing to complex statistical analyses, chances are, that
person can't stand you." Well, you get the joke! The point
is this: so what? If you know who you are, as a woman
and as a uniquely created child of God, what do you care
what other people think?

Remember: You are not responsible for their reac-
tion. You are only responsible for your action. If you
reach out to someone with love and concern, your con-
science can rest easy. You've done the right thing. If the
recipient is less than gracious, well, so be it.

Self-Isolation

While it's true that we often fail to reach out to others, the opposite is also true. If I don't let women into
my life, how can they reach out to me? The worst thing
for women is being alone. It goes against the way God
created us. That's why we're so frustrated. People can't
know how to help us if they don't know us. As Cynthia
Fantasia says, "You have to invest in relationship building before a crisis hits. Women will be much more inclined to reach out to you if a comfort level has already
been established. They need 'permission' to offer you
help."

"People who are socially lonely, tend to blame themselves for their isolation," according to Robert Weiss of
the University of Massachusetts in Boston (*Ladies Home
Journal*, April 1991). "They may harbor a feeling that
people don't like them—a sense that everyone was invited to the party but them." In my experience, this is
one of the toughest hurdles to overcome, especially for
stay-at-home moms. Everything in our culture bom-
bards us with the message that we are second rate, that
we have nothing interesting to offer. We buy into the lie,
and we're afraid to reach out. We're afraid of rejection,
so we sit in our homes alone. Not admitting our need.
Feeling confused and angry because "all the other moth-

ers have it together, why don't I?" In truth, the woman down the street is as plagued by self-doubt as you are. If you'll just reach out.

Cynthia continues, "Unfortunately, we set up these walls around us. One of the biggest challenges I face as head of a large women's ministry is: how do we teach women to take risks? A friend of mine had a poster in her college dormitory that read: 'If you don't want to cry, don't play the game.' Crying is part of life. Pain is part of life; it's the price we pay for the joys of friendship. And the joys are well worth the risks."

Fear and Mistrust

In a crime and abuse-ridden country, we are afraid to trust. As one mother said, "I was in a department store looking at something, when suddenly I realized my daughter was out of sight. I was absolutely panic-stricken, sure some monster had kidnapped her. But like any typical child, she was just exploring what's under those racks of clothes. The world is so dangerous today. My mom used to take us to the store and deposit us in the toy department while she shopped. Those days are long gone. Now I have to watch every move my kids make and it is exhausting." How can you reach out to someone else when you're so exhausted from maintaining a constant vigil over your own children?

Of course, the bogeyman not only lurks in stores, he lurks in neighborhoods. That friendly new woman on the block could be part of a child pornography ring. Or her husband could be some sick, twisted molester. Or her teenage son could decide to experiment on your precious child. We don't know our neighbors. And we're terrified when we discover we really didn't know neighbors we thought we knew.

The saddest part of all is our fears are justified. Research indicates one in four American girls will be sexually abused by the age of 18; the statistics for boys are not much better: one in seven. We have a right to fear for our children. We also have a responsibility to build relationships based on love and mutual commitment, because "perfect love drives out fear" (1 John 4:18).

The Macho-Mom Syndrome

This syndrome most often manifests itself in the stay-at-home mom, but moms who work outside can fall into this trap, too. Again, it comes back to a mother's need to prove her worth, to prove that she is still smart and capable even though she's taking care of small children.

Many mothers view their struggles as a rite of passage into true womanhood. They believe suffering is part of the game. If you don't believe me, get women talking about their labor stories, their colicky babies, their trips to the emergency room. (By the way, just thought I'd mention: I was in labor for nineteen hours and my daughter had colic for a year. Are you impressed?)

For some women, a vicious cycle develops shortly after she brings the baby home from the hospital. Once all the initial excitement dies down, she begins to experience the tremendous isolation that strikes almost all new mothers. The adjustment can be especially traumatic for a woman who's worked outside the home for many years and suddenly finds herself home alone. She's plagued by self-doubts and feels unworthy. Meanwhile, no one calls or stops by. They want her to have plenty of time to bond with her baby. The only way to end the cycle is to kiss the Macho Mom goodbye!

Lack of a Game Plan

Mothers want to unite. That's the feeling I get when I talk with women from all over the country. Their real problem is not just time constraints, self-imposed isolation, fear, mistrust, or even the Macho-Mom syndrome. Their real problem is the lack of a game plan. Never fear, help is here. You have in your hands an action-packed game plan to help you personally discover the advantages of joining forces with other mothers.

Take Time for Reflection

Part 1: Personal Evaluation

For each of the following factors discussed in this chapter, note how it has personally affected your sense of isolation. (If you don't feel isolated at home, you're a very lucky lady. Jump ahead to the next section.)

1. Mobility (far from home)

_____

_____

2. Time Constraints

_____

_____

3. Personal Insecurity

_____

_____

4. Self-Isolation (walls)

_____

_____

5. Fear and Mistrust

_____

_____

6. Macho-Mom Syndrome

_____

_____

Part 2: Taking Action

Here are some simple things you can do in the coming weeks to reach out to women in your church or neighborhood. Next to each suggestion you would like to try, list the name of the person and when you plan to do it. Use the blank lines to come up with additional ideas.

ACTIVITY	FOR	WHEN
Make an extra casserole	_____	_____
Pick up a gallon of milk	_____	_____
Take children to the park	_____	_____
Write a note of encouragement	_____	_____

4

United We Stand: The Advantages of Mothers' Support Networks

ENOUGH THEORY, let's meet some former Lone Ranger moms who've discovered creative and practical ways to support one another in the job of mothering. Through their firsthand experience, we'll discover the advantages of mothers' support networks.

Jeanie Barantas

Jeanie Barantas recalls the toughest part about her babysitting co-op was getting it off the ground. "The woman who jump-started our group had been involved with a co-op in her home state of Kansas. She was willing to put in the hard work, because she knew from experience it would be worth it." Jeanie found some mothers reluctant to commit, at first. And, as always, "no one wants to get the ball rolling for fear no one else will jump in. Then they'll look like a kook."

"It was scary," admits Jeanie. "Hey, I'd never done this before. But I know so many people are without the support system of extended family. You've got to create your own network. In the beginning, that's going to make your life more complicated. But in the long run, it'll make your life easier."

Jeanie used the babysitting co-op for roughly four hours per week, depending on how busy her life was. "For me, the really important thing was attending our monthly meetings. That kept me in touch and helped me get to know other women. No one wants to leave their child with a stranger."

Jeanie says one of the greatest benefits of her co-op was all the great cooks in the group. "We always provided each other with fantastic meals for four full weeks whenever someone became a new mom. When I gave birth to my daughter, five women came over and cleaned my whole house."

Another favorite activity of Jeanie's was called Sit and Play. "During the summer, we would trade off hosting a mini preschool. We had three moms in our group. Each week, one mom would entertain all the kids for a few hours, while the other two moms enjoyed time for themselves. We took turns and the kids really enjoyed it. So did the moms."

Jeanie's advice to other moms? "Stick your hand out and make a friend. Even if you start with only one other mom, it will be so worth the effort!"

Barbara Roby

Barbara, mother of four-year-old Laura and two-year-old Ryan, joined Las Madres shortly after the birth of her daughter. "I didn't have any family in the area. I felt very isolated and had no idea what I was doing. I heard about Las Madres through the hospital where Laura was born."

Las Madras unites mothers whose children were born during the same calendar year, according to neighborhood. There are now some 250 women meeting in small groups throughout various parts of California. They host monthly meetings with a guest speaker on educational topics such as child safety. Las Madras' Annual Fashion Show attracts more than 500 people. At the show, women sell crafts they have worked on throughout the year. A percentage of their earnings for the evening are donated back to the club. They also publish a newsletter.

Las Madres continues to grow because each chapter is responsible for forming a new chapter for mothers of younger children. "We host a tea and invite new mothers. We explain the concept and offer to help them start a new club," says Barbara. Las Madres has even prepared a handbook for starting a new club, which explains the ins-and-outs of start-up and operation. They also actively promote your network by posting flyers at libraries, hospitals, pediatricians' offices, childbirth classes, churches, the Y, and other places new or expectant moms might congregate. This large and highly organized network has a phone tree to keep communications flowing smoothly.

Barbara's network, called the 1990 Club (because all their children were born in 1990), meets in a church once a week for three hours. In addition to spending time together for their weekly playgroup, they organize zoo trips, train rides, beach days, even an annual visit to the pumpkin patch. They also plan both Moms' Night Out and Couples' Night on a regular basis. According to Barbara, one of the highlights was a Mom's weekend away at the beach.

Barbara enjoys the network because "It's good to meet other moms and find out how they cope. And to watch their children grow along with mine."

They also have a "Sunshine Mom" who keeps her ears open for problems. The Sunshine Mom will schedule meals if a member is sick, has a new child, or if there's a death in the family. She also makes sure everyone's birthday is acknowledged. It's exactly that kind of support that could bring sunshine into your life!

Lynn Murtagh-Hartge

Lynn has the distinguished honor of belonging to mothers' support networks in three states. Her first experience was with a babysitting co-op in Plymouth, Michigan. The co-op was just one function offered through the local Newcomers Club, which is a nationwide non-profit volunteer women's organization.

"I was a very new mom at the time," says Lynn. "The co-op members helped with my children while I attended to volunteer committees, luncheons, and enjoyed my involvement with the board of Newcomers. I relied on two other moms whom I felt particularly comfortable with to care for my son Sean, now four, and Sarah, now three." To choose mothers she wanted to co-op with, Lynn watched how they interacted with their own child and with hers while she was present. "I immediately eliminated women I observed carrying on their normal household duties while babysitting my child. Some mothers had older children and weren't as vigilant as I would have liked," admits Lynn. "I know I'm more particular than most. But I noticed that like-minded mothers with similar parenting styles naturally found each other. Also women with children in similar age groups tended to drift together."

When Lynn's husband was transferred to San Diego, she immediately connected with Las Madras. "Since I'd been involved with the Michigan group, I knew the importance of connecting with other mothers. It was especially important because I was new in town. They helped me with referrals to doctors, children's clothing stores, babysitters, and just finding out what was where.

"They gave me the friendship I needed in a new state 3,000 miles from my family. We started out as just a playgroup, but we grew from there. We had Moms' Night Out once a month when we would go out to dinner. It was nice to have a conversation without the kids needing our attention."

Lynn recalls, "My Thursday morning playgroup was the highlight of my week. As the women developed deep friendships, we wanted to know the whole family. The missing piece was our husbands. So we planned mixer evenings so everyone could meet each other's husbands. We played crazy games and planned ice breaker activities. So, our group not only gave our children a chance to play together and socialize, it gave the couples an extended social life. It added a new dimension to our marriages, because now the couples could do things together. It was something we had in common."

Out of the initial network, Lynn found a best friend and they've kept in touch even though Lynn has since moved away. Altogether, there are four women she continues to keep in touch with and will always consider good friends.

Now Lynn is bringing the support network concept to her new home of Mesa, Arizona. "Probably the first thing I did was try to connect with a mothers' group. I contacted the Southeast Valley Women's Club, looking for a playgroup. The woman I talked with explained that her organization didn't have one, but she knew of another woman who might be interested. I called her and we started with just our two families."

Over the past two years, the playgroup has grown to nine mothers with fifteen children ranging in age from one to five years. "Whenever I meet mothers on the street, or at the park, I encourage them to join us. I carry flyers with me at all times. If I meet a neat lady, I give her one."

Lynn's group meets on Friday mornings at 11:30. "We try never to go to the same place twice. We keep it changing, so it stays fresh. Every other week, we go to a park. On the other weeks, we go on an outing, like the zoo or out for pizza, or a puppet show. Even though the women are from a fairly wide geographic area, we make the effort to get together because the group is meaningful to us. Since the weather is nice here in Arizona, outdoor meetings work great and we don't have to clean up afterwards."

Lynn says when the network gets a bit larger, they'll divide up by geography or by age or a combination of the two, similar to the approach used by Las Madres. She says the key to keeping women enthused is creating fun activities. "You also have to realize not everyone is a doer. Only a small percentage will get the work done, but that's okay. Let people join you where they are."

Carol Gurrola

In her life B.C. (before children), Carol Gurrola and her husband belonged to a Friday night Bible study for many years. When the five couples began transforming into families, they decided to move beyond talk to provide practical help for one another.

"Suddenly, we all had new responsibilities and new pressures as the children came along. Although our friendships were very close and everyone would say, 'Call me anytime' and 'I'll gladly take the kids,' no one asked for help. We were afraid we were imposing."

All that changed when one of the mothers took the initiative to set up the Santa Clarita Co-op. "It made all the difference in the world to have a formal system in place. We typed up a roster including all the mothers who wanted to participate. Then we assigned a secretary to keep track of our babysitting hours. We assigned one point per child per hour and a half point for a second child. If you served a meal, that was worth one quarter point. You could also earn one quarter point if you picked the children up or met the mom halfway. That was important for our group, because some of us lived fifteen miles away. The 'dropping' mom would lose points, the sitting mom would gain points.

"We had an official meeting every two months. That's when we took a hard look at who had been babysitting and who hadn't! It's also time for someone else to take a turn at being secretary." At its peak, ten mothers were actively involved.

Today, Carol, a registered nurse, devotes her time to childbirth training and caring for her two children: Andrew, nine, and Christina, six.

Susan Fletcher

Susan Fletcher is a veteran of many mothers' support networks: some have worked extremely well and others haven't worked at all. She shares her insight: "In order for it to work, the group has to be very structured and organized. I was in one for seven years and it is still going strong. If it's informal and casual, one person ends up doing all the sitting and things just fade out. I've seen it go both ways. I've been involved in both church-based and community-based support networks. It works best within the context of a neighborhood, at least that's been the case in my experience."

Active in several playgroups, Sue says, "First, you have to be bold enough to look for opportunities and to stick out your hand and say Hi. But you also need to be easy to relate to. Other women need to see you as the not-so-perfect mom, because they are not any more perfect. Then we can all breathe a sigh of relief. Let your neighbors or friends see the disaster in your kitchen once in a while. Confess that sometimes you have really 'lost it—BIG TIME' with the kids. I hate to admit how many times I dashed around cleaning things up because someone from my babysitting co-op was coming over to drop her kids off. All because I didn't want them to know the truth about my inadequacies as a housekeeper."

Sue continues, "The point is that we all have our not-so-gracious moments and in order to help each other, we need to not hide behind a false image of perfection and an 'I can handle it all' attitude. We don't have to play Supermom. I have been most drawn to women with whom I have felt free to be fallible, to be far less than perfect, but all of us still striving to become better. We draw strength, comfort, and encouragement from knowing others have struggled . . . and survived. I am so thankful for women with whom I have developed relationships where it is okay to ask for help. And I especially appreciate the relationships where I don't **NEED** to ask for help.

"When my fourth child was born, my **MOPS** discussion group decided the best gift they could give me was to come over and clean my house. They knew that was my biggest struggle because we had all been honest with each other.

"Even though it's scary at first, try being open and honest about your needs. In the long run, it is much easier than pretending that it is all so easy and you've got it all together."

Thanks to the support Susan received from her support network—and one woman in particular—she was able to finish her master's degree. Today, she is the mother of four children: Corey, nine, Kevin, seven, Laura, five, and Jeffrey, three.

Summing Up the Advantages

After listening to Jeanie, Barbara, Lynn, Carol, and Susan tell their stories, you probably have a good handle on what the advantages of a mothers' support network are. Let's just sum it up:

Getting out of the house. What is it about just plain getting out of the house that puts motherhood in perspective? Is it the sunshine? The fresh air? Maybe it's the realization that life goes on, even when our children's rooms are a disaster; even when last night's dinner dishes are still waiting in the sink; even when we lose our temper. The world keeps turning, and tomorrow promises another chance to try again.

I remember the long winter months, growing up in Philadelphia, when we were stuck indoors so much of the time. We kids would be bouncing off the walls, which was a lot of fun for Mom, who had eight of us to chase after. She called the gloomy, crazy mood in our house 'cabin fever.' And that's exactly what many moms today suffer from. When the outer limit of your universe is the pile of laundry in the basement, your problems appear much larger than they really are.

Whatever it is, moms need to get out of the house. And joining forces with other moms in your neighborhood is the perfect way to make sure you do exactly that.

Friendships with other young mothers. The common thread among all the mothers interviewed for this book is the joy of the friendships they formed through their mothers' groups. When you share the experience of motherhood with another woman, it creates a bond like few others you'll ever experience in your lifetime. It's the kind of bond men feel with the men who served alongside them on the battlefield. Come to think of it, it's exactly the same feeling. Because trying to raise good children today puts mothers right in the middle of the civil war of values. In a war that intense, you can use all the friends you can get.

If you stepped into motherhood fresh from the working world, one of the hardest adjustments is leaving behind your working buddies. Although everyone insists you'll stay in touch, the truth is, you are now living in two separate worlds. And no matter how hard you try, it's tough to find common ground. That's why forming new friendships, especially with mothers in your own neighborhood, is so important.

Companionship for your children. In a survey I conducted while researching this book, the number one reason women cited for joining a mothers' support network was "to find companions for my children to play with." Many people promote preschool as the ideal way for children to learn socialization skills. However, many of the women I interviewed believe the socialization of their children is something they need to monitor carefully. In other words, your child could easily learn the *wrong* way to interact with other children.

As Ann Meo notes, "Because so many children these days are in daycare or preschool, children at home with their mothers don't have as much chance to play with other children. You can't just send your kids out to play, like the good old days when we were growing up. Now, it's up to the moms to make an extra effort to find playmates for their children."

Hopefully, this won't sound too judgmental, but I must admit there are some children I don't want Leah to play with—at least, not without me present to supervise what's going on. Sadly enough, there are four-year-old children who use profanity, who hit, who show no respect for adults or other children. I don't want Leah to get the idea that such behavior is acceptable. Although I certainly don't want to exclude any neighborhood children, I also need to guard my daughter's mind and spirit. With a parent-led playgroup, I can do exactly that.

Chance to build couple friendships. As many moms can attest, when you choose to stay at home with your children, it's almost like you and your husband are living in two different worlds. As one woman noted, "With so many corporations downsizing and expecting the remaining employees to get more work done, many husbands are just too exhausted to go out and pursue friendships. And yet, it's so important for them to have male friends. One of the unexpected benefits of our group is that my husband, Mark, has become friends with the other husbands.

"These couple friendships are important, because they give us yet another thing in common. We can talk about activities we've done together as couples. And when I talk about so-and-so from the co-op, or a child I sat for today, he knows who I'm talking about. He's part of my world. I think that can only strengthen our marriage."

Joy of watching your children grow alongside other children. One of the great joys of participating in a mothers' support network has been watching Leah and the other children grow up together. It's been a delight to see our children's relationships blossom from the parallel play stage into genuine friendships. I'll never forget the first time Leah fell victim to a clique in the playgroup. It was during a Valentine's Day party. Two little four-year-old girls she frequently played with informed Leah that they were playing with each other ONLY—Leah just wasn't part of the plan. When I saw Leah's tears, I couldn't help remembering times when I, too, was the "odd man out" on the playground.

I introduced Leah to another little girl and got the two of them interested in making birthday cakes out of sand. We were having great fun, when along came the two "clique" members. Suddenly, everyone was friends again and we had survived our first social trauma! The situation resolved, I went and sat on the sidelines while the girls laughed and played together. What a moment!

Reality check. Participating in a support network also helps during those not-so-joyous moments of motherhood. Like when your son creates a mural on his bedroom wall with black magic marker. Or when your four-year-old suddenly "forgets" to get up and go to the bathroom at night. As Ann Meo says, "I used to think I was the only mom in the world who couldn't take my children to a restaurant."

There's a certain comfort when you realize your kids aren't the only ones who seem to take a sinister delight in publicly humiliating you, or that you're not the only mom who sometimes loses her cool. During one of our recent 6:00 A.M. walks, Susan confided her most embarrassing moment as a mom. "I took Jason [two years old] with me to get a photograph for my driver's license. Well, he decided it would be fun to swing around on the turnstile. So, of course, I told him no way. At which time, he threw himself on the floor and started screaming at the top of his lungs. No matter what I tried to do, it didn't work. Finally, this great big woman behind the counter gave me this glaring look and said, 'Lady, if you can't get your child under control, you'll have to leave the premises.' As I dragged my screaming child out the door, I thought I was going to die of embarrassment."

With that, I and the other woman in our "walking club" burst into laughter and started telling her about OUR humiliating motherhood experiences. Susan realized she wasn't the only one, and we knew it, too. It may not put an end to our children's antics, but it can certainly put our minds at ease.

Activities for kids you wouldn't plan alone. In the last few months, our group has taken the children to a dairy farm, a fire station, a puppet show, an indoor playground, a swim club, and a special children's reading hour at a local bookstore. Be honest, now, how many of you moms could have—or would have—planned all those activities for your children? Did you raise your hand? Okay, could you plan all that for your children and *still have a life for yourself?* No way. That's the power of networking. Each of these events were planned by a different mom, for the benefit of all the children.

Activities for you, which you probably wouldn't do alone. Speaking of activities you wouldn't ordinarily do, when's the last time you went to a jazz concert under the stars? When's the last time you and ten other moms laughed over dinner at an Italian restaurant? When's the last time you invaded a miniature golf course with fifteen of your friends? More to the point, when's the last time you went to such places . . . without your kids? Women in our network have done all that and more.

I don't know about you, but there is no way I would have taken the initiative to do any of those things. As Anita Wingfield put it, "As we mothers can all attest to, time to yourself or with other women is vital. But it's usually the last item on a long list of priorities. To have social activities preplanned and already on my calendar is a big incentive to make that time just for myself. For me personally, these times out alone help me feel like my own person and not just 'Ryan's mom' or 'Mark's wife.' "

Another network member, Jennifer Reinholtz, has noticed yet another benefit of our Moms' Night Out. "It lets our children spend a night with Dad all alone. That's something stay-at-home moms may forget to let Dad do." And it sure helps Dad to appreciate all the hard work you do as a mom.

What are you waiting for? Get your own network started, leave the kids home with Dad and go enjoy yourself. It's Moms' Night Out!

Opportunity to pursue personal interests or career goals. We mothers pour so much of ourselves into our children, which is great. Yet, it's also good to occasionally have time to pursue our own interests. Even though the days sometimes seem to last forever, mothers who've been there constantly remind me, "the years go by so fast." The day will come when your children will leave the nest. The adjustment will be much easier—for both you and your children—if you've maintained your own identity throughout the mothering years. A solid support network gives you the freedom to do that.

Susan Fletcher was actually able to finish her master's degree with the support of her network. How many mothers of preschoolers could accomplish that on their own? Not very many!

Several mothers in my network, especially Ann, Anita, and Diane, were instrumental in my being able to write this book and still be a half-decent wife and mommy. Still others are able to pursue a home-based business on the side, or work out at the gym without hiring a babysitter.

And those are just a few of the advantages of building your own support network. I'll bet you can think of many more.

Take Time for Reflection

1. On a scale of 1 to 10, with 10 meaning extremely important, rate how important each of the following advantages are to you.

Getting out of the house	10 9 8 7 6 5 4 3 2 1
Friendships with other mothers	10 9 8 7 6 5 4 3 2 1
Companionship for your children	10 9 8 7 6 5 4 3 2 1
Chance to build couple friendships	10 9 8 7 6 5 4 3 2 1
Watching children grow with friends	10 9 8 7 6 5 4 3 2 1
Reality check	10 9 8 7 6 5 4 3 2 1
Activities kids wouldn't otherwise do	10 9 8 7 6 5 4 3 2 1
Activities you wouldn't otherwise do	10 9 8 7 6 5 4 3 2 1
Opportunities to pursue personal goals	10 9 8 7 6 5 4 3 2 1

2. For each of the items you rated higher than 8, list an action step you can take in the next week to begin experiencing that advantage in your life:

ADVANTAGE	ACTION STEP
_____	_____
_____	_____
_____	_____
_____	_____
_____	_____

3. Go back over the list, but this time think about the

needs of other women in your life. How can you serve as a vehicle to help them enjoy the various benefits of a mothers' support network?

NAME	ADVANTAGE	ACTION STEP TO ASSIST THEM
_____	_____	_____
_____	_____	_____
_____	_____	_____
_____	_____	_____
_____	_____	_____

4. List activities you would like to do, but never take the time to do (examples: hiking, weekend at the beach, dinner with friends, day of pampering at a spa). Don't worry about the logistics, just jot down whatever comes to mind, from the simple to the exotic.

_____

_____

_____

_____

_____

5. Pick the activity that most appeals to you, and begin laying plans to turn your idea into reality. If you are working through this book in a group, compare lists. Join forces with women who listed similar ideas.

TOP PICK: _____

WHEN: _____

WHERE: _____

WHO ELSE: _____

HOW (List Action Steps):

_____

_____

_____

_____

_____

6. List activities you have great intentions of doing with your children, but never get around to doing (examples: art museums, exhibits, library reading hour, picnics). Again, jot down any ideas that come to mind:

_____

_____

_____

7. Pick the one that most appeals to you, and begin laying plans to turn your idea into reality. If you are working through this book in a group, compare lists. Join forces with women who listed similar ideas.

TOP PICK: _____

WHEN: _____

WHERE: _____

WHO ELSE: _____

HOW (List Action Steps):

_____

_____

_____

_____

8. List some personal goals you would like to pursue, but can't seem to find the time for (examples: learning a new skill, taking a college class, serving your church or community).

_____

_____

_____

_____

_____

_____

9. Once again, compare notes with the other women in your network. Discuss ways that you can support one another in pursuing personal goals while keeping motherhood a priority.

PART TWO

THE SOLUTION

5
Church-Based and Community-Based Networks

THROUGHOUT THE BOOK, I give examples of both church-based and community-based support networks. Let's take a look at the advantages and disadvantages of both.

The Church-Based Network

Becky Albrecht feels passionately about the importance of the church-based network. "The church is where it needs to happen. This is the place where mothers should come to feel loved and cared for. The church is where unconditional love can happen. At our church (Immanuel Presbyterian of Exton, Pennsylvania), we don't have a director of women's ministry. We believe that gives women the wrong idea, that caring for one another has to be a paid position. Or they think the only time we should get together is for a formal, carefully planned event. For the most part, we support each other on a very informal basis."

Support is an understatement for the way women at Immanuel Presbyterian care for one another. When I lived on the East Coast, I heard many reports about these terrific women. Their self-sacrifice and love were legendary throughout area churches.

"The really exciting thing," says Becky, "is when women from the community come into our network. They say, 'Wow, you women really care about each other. This is new to me.' And they want to become part of what we're doing. Our weekly Bible studies attract women from many different churches and women who don't go to church at all. We think that's the way it should be."

Although Becky and the other women of Immanuel Presbyterian believe practical support should take place within the context of the church, they certainly don't limit their concern. In fact, they actively look for opportunities to help other women in their neighborhood. For example, Becky recalls, "There was a woman we learned about who was in danger of having a miscarriage. She wasn't part of our church, in fact, I didn't even know her. Most of us hadn't even met her before. She was a friend of one of the women at our church, so we all began preparing meals for her family."

At the time, Becky had four children of her own, but she was willing to reach out. "I took my baby with me and dropped off the other three at a friend's house. When I arrived the woman was on the phone; she said to the person on the other end of the line: 'This one came with a bucket.'" Becky marched directly to the bathroom and set to work.

Becky is very big on buckets. So are the rest of the women at Immanuel Presbyterian. When they arrive to deliver a meal to someone—whether there's an illness, a new baby, or whatever—the women will almost always ask: "Can I dust while I'm here? Can I clean your bathroom? How about the kitchen?" Whenever possible, the woman who delivers the meal will try to arrange to clean up after dinner. Whether that means staying (and working) while the family eats or coming back when they have finished.

"We have a saying at our church: 'Greater love has no woman than to lay down her cleanser in the bathroom of a friend.' Whenever there's a new baby or someone sick in bed, we head directly for the bathroom because that's the toughest job in the house. We also mop kitchen floors. But the woman in need has to be willing to admit that her kitchen floor is dirty.

"I hope this doesn't sound judgmental," says Becky, "but I honestly don't believe that many women outside the church would be willing to do these kinds of things. At least, I haven't seen women in our society showing that kind of love. I really think you have to be motivated by God's love or you'll quickly get tired of doing good."

Becky believes: "The real serving doesn't begin until it's inconvenient. It's watching each other's children beyond what's a good time for me. It's saying, 'That's NOT a good time for me, but I'll do it anyway.' It's choosing to make the inconvenient, convenient.

"Anyone can be committed for the short-term, but what about the long-term?" she asks. When Becky's neighbor Dawn was in the hospital awaiting a bone marrow transplant, the women of the church rallied around her. "We donated blood and prepared meals for her family. We continued caring for them for months. We were willing to inconvenience ourselves."

On another occasion, Becky's family invited a pregnant nineteen-year-old girl to live with them. The challenges turned out to be more than they could bear, but again, the women in the church got involved. They invited her for meals, took the time to befriend her. They even organized a baby shower when the time approached.

"When another woman was expecting twins, representing her sixth and seventh children, we all pitched in to provide meals, clean her house, and care for her children," Becky recalls. "No one passed judgment on her or said, 'Gee, why did you get pregnant again when you can't handle the ones you've got?' Instead, we gave her unconditional support for as long as she needed it." Becky herself has seven children: Tom, sixteen; Matt, thirteen; Steve, twelve; Elizabeth, nine; Mark, seven; Andrew, five, and Peter, three.

Whenever Becky or another woman learns of someone in need, a member of the church is assigned to keep a calendar of meals, etc., to ensure the person gets the help they need. They present the opportunity to serve and the women respond by signing up. If for some reason all the dates are not covered, whoever is keeping the calendar will call around and recruit women to fill the need. In general, however, women take the initiative to contact her and volunteer to sign up. Becky observes, "Most women really want to help, but they need a place to plug in. By providing opportunities for women to make a difference in other people's lives, we believe we're getting to the very heart of what the church is all about."

The Advantages of the Church-Based Network

1. Relatively easy to launch the network, because you have a ready-made core of women to draw upon.
2. Instant publicity through the Sunday bulletin and church bulletin boards. The network can also be promoted through existing women's groups and Bible studies.
3. Communications about events, concerns, etc., are easier because women see each other regularly.

4. Automatic access to facilities for meetings, cooking, special events, etc.

5. Women already know and, ideally, trust one another. They'll be more inclined to jump right in with network activities.

6. Women will have shared values and belief systems.

7. In many cases, women will have a similar child-rearing philosophy and approach to discipline.

8. When problems arise, you have an agreed upon standard (the Bible) with which to resolve the situation.

9. You can pray together as a group—an excellent way to put petty problems into perspective.

The Disadvantages of the Church-Based Network

1. Many churches today attract members from a diverse geographic area. It's hard to hold a network together when the women do not live within close range of one another.

2. There's a danger that women will not reach out beyond their own network, but will become too inwardly focused. That's not what the church is supposed to be about.

3. Many mothers in the church are already very active. They may be reluctant to take on additional activities.

4. The women may begin spending too much time together, with both church and network activities, and start to get on each other's nerves! (We speak only the truth here.)

The Community-Based Network

"Geography is king," according to Judy Pfaff of San Jose, California. She's an active member of the community-based network Las Madres and serves as director of her local playgroup. Judy insists the ideal network is one that operates within the close quarters of a local neighborhood.

"I want to connect with mothers right here in my neighborhood, where I live and where my children play each day. One of the most important things about Las Madres is that it is rebuilding the sense of community that seems to be missing in most places today."

Judy's group, in the Willow Glen section of San Jose, includes twenty-four moms, most of whom have two children. All of the women live within close proximity of one another and all of them have a child born during 1990. "We definitely have a lot in common, so we have no trouble finding things to talk about," says Judy. The group meets every Thursday at a park or other activity site for about two and a half hours.

Within their sub-group of Las Madres, they have sub-sub-groups. For example, they have a "Sit and Play" which meets on Tuesdays for three hours. Here's how it works: six mothers bring their children to the designated house. Two mothers stay to entertain the twelve children while the other four moms are free to do whatever they want. They meet at a different house every week.

They also have a babysitting co-op, which includes thirteen women. They use the Secretary system, where one mother serves as coordinator for the month. If someone needs a sitter, she contacts the acting secretary who then calls the member with the most negative hours and asks her to babysit. If that person is unavailable, she'll contact the member who has the second most negative hours, and so on. The Acting Secretary keeps a central log of everyone's hours. When the sitter is done, she calls and reports how many hours she served. The secretary deducts the hours from the gadder (a term that refers to the mother who drops her child(ren) off to be babysat by another member, who is called the sitter) and adds them to the sitter.

The babysitting co-op is extremely active. Judy reports using it an average of fifteen hours per month for her two children, Janelle, three, and Brian, twenty months. "I use it because it's convenient. If I had to travel across town just to drop my kids off so I could go grocery shopping in peace, I wouldn't bother. But since I can take them just a few blocks away, it's worth it," she says.

Judy's group organizes a wide range of special projects. "Once a month, we get together at someone's house for Craft Night. The dads stay home and take care of the kids, which is great," she says. Sometimes they have an organized craft session; other times, each woman brings whatever craft or sewing item she's been working on lately. "It's an opportunity to work on simple tasks while the moms enjoy socializing. It's just like the old quilting parties. You've got to do this stuff anyway, so why not get the job done while enjoying the companionship of other women." Again, she stresses, "Who would go to Craft Night if it was on the other side of town? Since it's down the street, we all go."

Craft Night is also an opportunity for women to share their special talents or interests with one another. For example, one woman taught eight others how to do rubber stamping. "We made really practical items, like invitations for kids' parties, birth announcements, greeting cards. We also created beautiful stationery to give as gifts. We enjoyed it so much, now we have a rubber stamp party every three months or so. Each of the women brings her stamps and we all share. So we save money and enjoy a greater variety of creations. One very popular rubber stamp series was botanicals—there was a rose, iris, tulip, etc. Rather than each of us going out and buying them all, we coordinated our shopping and each woman bought a different one. Rather than spending $80 each, we spent only $10 each."

Why has Las Madres been wildly successful while similar groups have failed? Judy believes there are two major factors: organization and convenience. "It works because it is very organized. Each of the sub-groups has to report to the Las Madres leadership, so there is some accountability. There are established procedures for everything, so you know exactly what to do to make your network successful. There's no guesswork, no trial-and-error. Over time, Las Madres has discovered what works and everyone goes by it.

"The second reason it works is because it's so convenient. We assign women to groups right in their own community, so they don't have to travel very far to get involved. That's really important, because mothers don't want to drag their kids all over town just to be part of a playgroup. They don't want to drive forty-five minutes each way for a three-hour Sit and Play or travel a long distance for monthly meetings. Las Madres makes it easy and worthwhile to stay involved."

The Advantages of the Community-Based Network

1. The greatest advantage may be the most compelling one. Close proximity of members makes participation more convenient. And the more convenient it is to be part of the network, the more likely mothers are to stick with it over the long run.
2. It's easier to get everyone together, especially on short notice.
3. It's hard for mothers to make excuses not to participate. Who can't walk to the corner park?
4. Communication is easy, because flyers can be quickly delivered door to door.
5. Mothers who live in the same neighborhood usually have similar values and priorities—that's why they've chosen to live there.
6. Most families will be from the same socio-economic group. That's important when planning activities. Groups from more affluent neighborhoods can plan events like a ski weekend or other expensive activities, while groups in less pricey neighborhoods will want to plan more affordable outings. What's nice about the

neighborhood approach is that, rich or poor, chances are most everybody's in the same boat. That is not necessarily the case in a church group.

The Disadvantages of the Community-Based Network

1. It's harder to get the network off the ground, unless you have an established network of mothers.
2. More costly to promote than a church network, which has access to the church copy machine, Sunday bulletins, etc.
3. No instant access to facilities for meetings and special events. You'll have to rely on members' homes and public meeting places.
4. Neighborhood mothers may not feel the same depth of commitment to one another as mothers in a church might feel. (Although that is not necessarily the case, of course.)
5. Potential religious incompatibility and/or widely divergent value systems.
6. A broad range of child-rearing philosophies and approaches to discipline.
7. May be too close for comfort!

Take Time for Reflection

1. What do you think are the advantages and disadvantages of starting a network in your community?

Advantages   Disadvantages

_____   _____

_____   _____

_____   _____

_____   _____

_____   _____

2. If you are part of a local church, list what you believe will be the advantages and disadvantages of launching a network at your church.

Advantages   Disadvantages

_____   _____

_____   _____

_____   _____

_____   _____

_____   _____

3. Which option do you prefer? Circle one:
Church-Based   Community-Based

6
What Type of Mom Are You?

IT TAKES ALL KINDS of women to make a mothers' network work. Yet, the very differences that create balance and wholeness can create conflict. (More on resolving conflict in Chapter 13.) Understanding why people act the way they do can go a long way toward promoting harmony. To that end, numerous philosophers, psychologists, and theologians have developed theories of personality to explain why we do what we do. The oldest system was developed by the ancient Greeks, who divided people into the four temperaments: Choleric, Sanguine, Phlegmatic, and Melancholy.

More recently, Lee Ellis, Director of Career Pathways, developed a system based on the DISC (Dominant, Influencing, Steady, and Conscientious) personality assessment system. The following charts are adapted from his book *Your Career in Changing Times* (Moody Press, 1993), coauthored with Larry Burkett. I'm also indebted to Mariette Holland, founder of PAX Seminars, for her insight and assistance with this portion of the book.

As you work through the charts and review the characteristics of each type of mom, be sure to focus on the positive. Don't use this information as a weapon against other women or as a way to label them with negative characteristics. Instead, your goal is to bring out the very best in others, while being the very best *you* possible.

You might find it especially effective to have each woman in your network complete the chart to determine what type of mother she is. Share this information openly, and actively strive to capitalize on each other's strengths. At the same time, understand that *everyone* has weaknesses . . . including you. Understanding the kind of mother you are will provide insight into how and why other people sometimes misunderstand you.

PERSONALITY CHART

Rate yourself by placing a dot on the vertical scale, 10 means you are very extroverted and 0 means you are very introverted. Put another dot on the horizontal scale, 10 means you are very formal, while 0 means you are very informal. When you're finished rating, connect the dots. I've rated a very formal and extroverted mom in the sample chart. The interpretation of your chart is on the following page. No peeking!

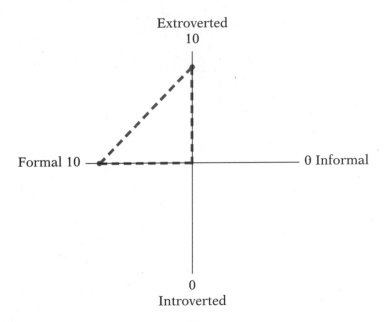

PERSONALITY KEY

You've just plotted your personality type. The larger the triangle you formed when connecting your dots, the stronger the characteristic is in you. Now, read on to find out the strengths and weaknesses associated with your type. Lee Ellis provides the following overview of the four behavioral tendencies.

D=*Dominant.* "Mothers who have a high level of dominance are naturally motivated to control their environments," says Ellis. "They are usually assertive, independent, confident, pioneering, direct, and strong-willed. They are typically bold and not afraid to take strong action to get the desired results. They are very driven to reach specific goals. They function best in a challenging environment." This type of mother is the "Take-Charge Mom."

I=*Influencing.* "Mothers who are highly influencing are naturally driven to relate to others," according to Ellis. "Usually they are talkative, gregarious, friendly, persuasive, fun-loving, and optimistic. They are typically enthusiastic motivators and will seek out others to help them accomplish results. They are also high-spirited and usually quite popular. Tending to be more emotional, they function best in a favorable environment." This is the "Fun Mom."

S=*Steady.* "Mothers who have a high level of steadiness are naturally motivated to cooperate with and support others," explains Ellis. "They are usually patient, consistent, considerate, loyal, and very dependable. Being pleasant and easygoing makes them excellent team players. They are especially productive when working in a supportive environment." This is the "Attentive Mom."

C=*Conscientious.* "Mothers with a high level of conscientiousness (or cautiousness) are focused on doing things right," says Ellis. "Usually they are detail-oriented, reserved, self-disciplined, and find it easy to follow prescribed guidelines. These mothers follow a careful schedule and maintain a very organized home. Typically they strive for accuracy and quality and, therefore, set high standards for themselves and others." They function best in a structured environment. She's the "Meticulous Mom."

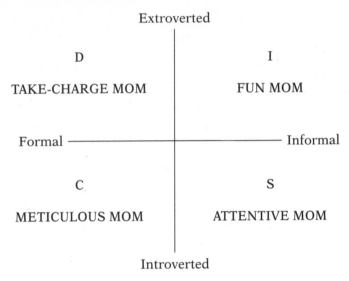

Each of the personality types has both strengths and weaknesses. None is better than another. None is more important to the success of your network. What is critical to the success of your network is understanding who's who and why they act the way they do. As Mariette Holland notes, "Learn to read which type of person you are dealing with, so you can give her what she needs and adapt your style accordingly." The following guidelines will get you started:

Interacting With the Take-Charge Mom

Making the most of her strengths. If you want to get a job done, ask the Take-Charge Mom to take control of the situation. And will she ever! She'll quickly set goals and make decisions, rather than waiting around to see

100

what's popular. She'll do more than keep busy, she'll actually get things done. You never have to wonder what the Take-Charge Mom is really thinking or feeling; she'll let you know right up front. She's a great problem-solver and can fix whatever is broken with the utmost of confidence—even if she has never faced that particular set of circumstances before.

You can count on the Take-Charge Mom to bounce back when things go wrong in the group. If one activity bombs, she'll just think up another and pursue it with equal vigor. And you can count on her to constantly introduce new ideas and enthusiastically initiate new projects. Her energy seems almost unlimited, and her ability to get things done is remarkable.

She likes to win, to be the best, and she'll work hard to make sure your mothers' network is the best it can be. And because the Take-Charge Mom is a visionary, she'll be able to determine what's best, not only in the short term but down the road as well. As long as she can keep her urge to control under control, she can make an excellent leader for your network.

Understanding her weaknesses. Problems start with the Take-Charge Mom when she tries to take *too* much control of the network, which the other mothers may resent. She can be quite the dictator. She has a tendency to act first and think things through afterward. This can really cause trouble if she initiates projects without making a realistic assessment of how much time and effort will be required to complete them. The Take-Charge Mom is great at getting things started; she's not so great at finishing. She tends to jump from project to project and leave the detailed clean-up work and follow-through to others—a fact that other mothers may also resent. And because she's overly demanding, she expects others to finish up quickly.

She can be overbearing and inconsiderate of other mothers' feelings. For example, she'll move ahead with new projects without seeking the advice or approval of others. She loves to talk but tends to forget that other people have important things to say, too.

Interacting With the Fun Mom

Making the most of her strengths. Who can resist the Fun Mom? Her bright cheery smile and her bubbly personality make her the life of the party. And does she ever like parties. She likes to throw them and she likes to attend them. She loves to laugh and can have a good time doing just about anything.

The Fun Mom can talk to anyone, anywhere, at any time, about almost anything. The eternal optimist, she always expects the best from people and from life. She's a trusting soul, who sees only the best in others and is quick to overlook people's weaknesses.

Thanks to her incredible verbal skills, she's great at persuading others to her point of view. When she feels passionately about a cause, she can easily win people to her side and inspire them to get involved. She's the ultimate "promoter." She's also the consummate networker and actively cultivates contacts who can help with various tasks. She's the mom to call if you're new in town—she can tell you exactly where to go for what and who to talk to.

Pray for as many Fun Moms as you can get, because they brighten up the network just by walking into the room. Best of all, everyone will claim the Fun Mom as their very best friend.

Understanding her weaknesses. Although the Fun Mom will do a great job of attracting new members and keeping everyone enthused, she may not be the ideal person to run the show. Why? Because she tends to be disorganized and rarely takes time for in-depth planning. She's easily distracted and has a tough time finishing what she starts.

The most common criticism of the Fun Mom, of course, is that she talks too much. She just can't stop talking! If you need to get in touch with her in a hurry, you'd better hope she has a voice-messaging system. Chances are she'll be talking on the phone whenever you call. You can never stop in her house for a minute. You have to allow at least an hour, because no matter what time of day or night it is, she'll want to chat. And chat. And chat. . . .

The Fun Mom can actually be so optimistic that she becomes just plain unrealistic. Also, she tends to be a poor judge of character because she takes people at face value, without looking at underlying motivations. She *needs* to be accepted and, therefore, finds it almost impossible to say no. As a result, she gets overcommitted and fails to follow through on her promises.

Also, the Fun Mom likes to try on new friends as much as she likes to try on new clothes. You'll think you've found your best friend for life, and without warning, she'll stop calling. She's too busy getting chummy with the new kid on the block. (Not that she doesn't love you anymore; it's just that she's got to go where something new and exciting is happening.) By the way, do not put her in charge of the treasury. Money flows through her hands like water. She'll have your network bankrupt in no time. (You'll have lots of fun on the way down, though!)

The Fun Mom can be a great leader, provided she serves in partnership with another mom who is more detail-oriented, like the Meticulous Mom.

Interacting With the Attentive Mom

Making the most of her strengths. The Attentive Mom has the corner on patience. She has her feet firmly rooted in reality and has a good sense of what it will take to get the job done. She also has the tenacity to stick with a project through to completion. The Attentive Mom is one hundred percent dependable—if she says she'll take care of something, it is as good as done.

This mom thrives on routine and you can bet she's got her child(ren) on a daily schedule that almost never varies. She goes about tasks in a consistent manner and doesn't follow after every new trend that comes along.

In terms of her interpersonal relationships, she thrives on harmony and will do whatever she can to maintain it. She'll adapt her working style to suit whoever she's with and is therefore the ultimate team player. Because she doesn't insist on having things go her way, she can get along with almost anyone.

The Attentive Mom is a very loyal friend and staunchly committed to her family. She's also a sympathetic listener, with a genuine concern for others. Chances are, the Attentive Moms in your network are the ones who will really get things done. If you need a reality-check, she's the one to see.

The Attentive Mom can be a great leader for your co-op, especially when a sure, steady hand is what's needed. However, she will probably prefer to play second-in-command and let someone else be the up-front person.

Understanding her weaknesses. If you're looking for someone to launch new programs and fire up your mothers' network, you'd better look elsewhere. The Attentive Mom prefers to stick with the tried-and-true. In fact, she'll even stick with the tried-and-found-lacking. She is slow to accept any kind of change in procedures and needs to recognize when it's time to abandon old methods.

The Attentive Mom also has a tendency to compromise too much and is reluctant to take a stand for what she believes in. She gets so caught up in the day to day details, she misses out on the big picture. Some Attentive Moms can be lazy, especially when it comes to pursuing goals.

Another danger with the Attentive Mom is the tendency toward bitterness. Sometimes she can be too self-sacrificing and overcommit herself. She's always there when everyone needs her, and she may begin to resent the fact that people are not as quick to meet her needs. She also has a strong need to be appreciated. If other women don't voice appreciation for her quiet efforts, she can feel taken advantage of and start playing the victim.

Interacting With the Meticulous Mom

Making the most of her strengths. The Meticulous Mom thrives on accuracy and aims for quality in everything she does. You can guess what her house looks like: sheer perfection. Her motto is "A place for everything and everything in its place." She's very detail-oriented and notices things that other people tend to overlook. She enjoys structure, discipline, and playing by the rules. Her children, no doubt, follow a set schedule each day.

If there's a job to be done, she'll go to any length to insure it is done properly. She has a very analytical mind and enjoys examining issues in detail. She arrives at her decisions with great care and deliberation; she never does anything rash.

Every mothers' network needs the steady hand of the Meticulous Mom. She's the voice of reason when things run amok.

Understanding her weaknesses. The Meticulous Mom can be just a little too perfect, and often she has unrealistic expectations of herself and others. And because she expects perfection, she's often disappointed and turns pessimistic. She tends to be very critical of herself and of other people. She's also highly sensitive, because she notices the slightest little affront. She has trouble forgiving and forgetting.

The Meticulous Mom is often so cautious and detail-oriented that it takes her forever to get things done. As Ellis notes, "She needs to realize there's not enough time to do everything perfectly and remember that some things only need a cursory effort."

But Who Is She?

Now that you have completed the chart and plotted your own personality, you have a good idea of what strengths and weaknesses you bring to your mothers' network. That should help you to become a more thoughtful and effective member. However, understanding yourself is only one piece of the puzzle. You also need to understand the women in your network—what makes each one tick.

The following chart provides you with clues to help you identify who's who. For example, how can you tell if a woman you have just met is an Attentive Mom or a Take-Charge Mom? Whether you meet her in a meeting or at the playground, there are specific behaviors you can look for. Once you understand who she is, you are in a better position to reach out and meet her needs.

Of course, no one fits exactly into these neat little categories. Every woman you meet is a uniquely created human being and there's no one on earth quite like her. In fact, Lee Ellis reports that only five to six percent of the population fit precisely into one of the DISC personality types. Most of us are a combination of two, with the most frequent combinations being D/I (Take-Charge/Fun Mom), D/C (Take-Charge/Meticulous Mom), S/D (Attentive/Take-Charge), and I/C (Fun/Meticulous Mom).

Nevertheless, these guidelines will give you greater understanding of the women around you. And when we reach out from a place of understanding, our efforts to demonstrate love and concern will be far more effective. If you would like to explore this subject in greater detail, I encourage you to read some of the books listed at the end of this chapter.

WHO'S WHO
CLUES TO LOOK FOR

	Meetings	Playground
TAKE CHARGE	She'll run the show—whether she's supposed to or not. And she'll get things done!	Are you kidding? She doesn't DO playgrounds. She'll delegate the job to someone else. Namely, the Attentive Mom.
FUN	She'll be talking, laughing, smiling, and just plain having fun.	She'll talk to every single person at the park, including the old man sitting on the bench. Then, she'll play on the swings.
ATTENTIVE	She'll make it a point to talk to moms who aren't part of the "in" crowd.	She'll bring a big Thermos and snacks to share. She'll constantly check to make sure no one goes hungry or thirsty.
METICULOUS	She'll quietly take careful notes on everything that happens.	She'll be busy checking the safety features of various playground equipment.

	Lunch pail	Phone	With her child
TAKE CHARGE	A perfectly balanced meal, packed the night before.	She'll leave detailed messages for you. When you call her, she'll take control of the conversation and you'll forget why you called in the first place. On the positive side, if you call her to take action on something, you can bet she'll get right to work. If it's ideas or solutions you're looking for, she'll offer hundreds!	Her child is carefully disciplined and usually very well behaved. She spells out exactly what she expects. Her consistent training often results in a self-confident and secure child.
FUN	Nothing. She'll give him money to buy fast food, cupcakes, and whatever else he wants.	You'll never get through, unless she has call waiting. In that case, you can expect your conversation (which will last at least one hour) to be interrupted every five minutes by another caller.	Discipline? What's that? She'll let her child just go with the flow and express himself. Her kid is the one bouncing off the walls and jumping on your couch.
ATTENTIVE	A goodie bag full of thoughtful surprises. Plus a little note card and stickers.	She'll call just to see how you're doing. If she thinks someone hurt your feelings at a recent event, you can bet she'll call to make peace.	Her child will be on her lap most of the time. As he grows older, she'll make sure he carries an apple to school for the teacher.
METICULOUS	Sandwiches cut into perfect triangles wrapped in plastic and aluminum foil for extra safety.	She'll ask detailed questions about everything you've said or done since you talked last. She will re-cap, word for word, any recent events. If you mention that your child is coughing, she'll have a checklist of 50 questions to determine the precise cause of the ailment.	She'll wake up the child to make sure he's sleeping okay. She's always talking to the child. She won't have much use for the babysitting co-op because she's the only one who can adequately take care of her child.

With your child

She'll discipline your child if she thinks he needs it, even if you are there! She'll send messages through your child: "Tell your mom I said so-and-so."

Best way to deal effectively with her

She wants you to show respect for her accomplishments. She especially likes to be acknowledged for her organizing skills. Let her delegate to you and make sure you follow through on your commitments. Get right to the point when you talk to her. She wants to know about results. Respect her time.

Your kids will come home and say, "I wish SHE was my mommy instead of you!"

Throw a party and invite her over. And let her be the star of the show. She loves to plan parties, but be ready to follow behind her to finish what she starts. Don't expect her to be your best friend forever...she'll be on to best friend #10,576. When she moves, your friendship is over. She's got a whole new circle of friends. Don't be envious when she moves on to her new friends.

If she's going to the park, she'll call to see if your child wants to go along. Especially if she fears your child is being left out.

She needs to be appreciated. Send her little encouraging notes, telling her you appreciate how hard she works. She loves unexpected attention. People have a tendency to take advantage of her. Don't place too many demands on her, because she can't say no, but she'll grow resentful.

If you want to drop off your child, you'd better leave a complete list of everyone you know, with phone numbers. What if such-and-such happens? When you pick up the child, she'll tell you, blow-by-blow, exactly what transpired.

She wants you to spend time with her, listening to her detailed stories. She's just the person to tell you who's the best doctor, the best dentist, etc. She likes being respected as a resource person. Ask her lots of questions, without adding your advice. If she asks you something, don't give her an off-the-cuff remark. She expects a thoughtful answer. Give her reasons.

Take Time for Reflection

1. WHAT TYPE OF MOM ARE YOU? Circle one.
Take-Charge   Fun   Attentive   Meticulous

2. List the strengths you bring to the network:

_____   _____

_____   _____

_____   _____

3. What weaknesses do you need to be sensitive to?

_____   _____

_____   _____

_____   _____

4. In the first column, list women in your network or potential members. (You can also do this for family members, friends, and anyone else with whom you want to strengthen your relationship.) In column two, make an educated guess concerning which personality type they fit into. In the third column, list three ways you will relate to them differently because of what you learned in this chapter.

NAME	TYPE	CHANGES YOU PLAN TO MAKE
_____	_____	_____
		_____
		_____
_____	_____	_____
		_____
		_____
_____	_____	_____
		_____
		_____
_____	_____	_____
		_____
		_____
_____	_____	_____
		_____
		_____
_____	_____	_____
		_____
		_____
_____	_____	_____
		_____
		_____
_____	_____	_____
		_____
		_____
_____	_____	_____
		_____
		_____

5. If you would like to investigate personality theory in greater detail, check out the following books:

> *Personality Plus*, by Florence Littauer (Fleming H. Revell, 1983).
> *Personality Puzzle*, by Florence and Marita Littauer (Fleming H. Revell, 1992).
> *Spirit-Controlled Temperament*, by Tim LaHaye (Tyndale House, 1966).
> *The Two Sides of Love*, by Gary Smalley and John Trent (Focus on the Family, 1990).
> *Understanding How Others Misunderstand You*, by Ken Voges and Ron Braund (Moody Press, 1991).
> *Your Career in Changing Times*, by Lee Ellis and Larry Burkett (Moody Press, 1993).

Although the following two books don't deal with personality theory per se, they are very helpful guides for promoting harmony in your network:

> *How to Get Along With Almost Anyone*, by H. Norman Wright (Word, 1989).
> *How to Win Friends and Influence People*, by Dale Carnegie (Simon and Shuster, revised 1981).

7
Why Women Should Play Football

I AM A FOOTBALL FANATIC. When I lived in Philadelphia, my Sunday afternoons during the winter were spent jumping, shouting, and cheering on the Philadelphia Eagles. When Coach Buddy Ryan left town, I was depressed for weeks. When I moved to Phoenix and the Cardinals recruited Coach Ryan a year later, I considered it a personal answer to prayer. I absolutely *love* football.

My brother, Dan, was a superb athlete all during our growing-up years. Since he is only eleven months older than I, I became his official cheerleader. No matter where the game was played, even hundreds of miles from home for a championship game, I would be there in the front row. I never missed a football or baseball game. But I did miss out on some important lessons. And I think a lot of other young girls did, too.

Although it is beginning to change in our culture, most of you were probably raised like I was. Boys learned to play team sports; girls learned to sit on the sidelines. Boys learned how to pull together to achieve a common goal; girls learned to compete for the boys' attention and approval. Boys learned to support, cheer for, and honor the strongest players on their team; girls learned to "cut the hotshots down to size" and to applaud conformity.

That's why men understand something many women have trouble grasping: that the team is only as good as the strongest and weakest player. To continue with the football analogy: Men idolize the quarterback and the fastest running back. Each man knows that the way the team wins is by making it easier for these star players to shine. They know the victory belongs to the entire team and there's enough glory to go around—*but first you've got to win.*

How do women treat the "quarterbacks" and the "leading touchdown scorers" on our teams? Do we work hard behind the scenes so they can shine—knowing that each member of the team has an important role to fulfill, even though some are more visible than others? Not on your life! We tackle our own quarterback. We trip up the fastest runners on our own team. Then we wonder why our team never wins the championship.

Of course, I am generalizing. Some men are lousy team players; and some women work wonderfully on teams. However, in my experience—in the corporate world, as an entrepreneur, and in women's groups—I've found that women have a tough time with the concept of teamwork.

What's all this talk about football and teamwork got to do with Lone Ranger moms? Simply this: the absence of team spirit is probably one of the biggest obstacles you will face when building your own support network. Many women don't buy into the "all for one and one for all" theory; they are much more likely to ask "what's in it for me right now?" That's the reality. Nevertheless, there are some positive steps you can take to promote teamwork among women.

Aim for One Hundred Percent Involvement

While it is true that not all women are go-getters or "doers," every woman in your network can and should get things done. She may not want to host the event, but she can surely bring the paper plates. She may not feel comfortable talking to new members, but she can photocopy the monthly newsletter that keeps everyone up-to-date.

Get people actively involved from the first day you begin organizing your own support network—whether it's with one other woman or fifteen people who call in response to a press release. Why? Because involvement equals ownership. When people devote their time and energy to something, they have a vested interested in seeing it succeed. It strengthens commitment, in both large and small things. Even in a simple thing like meeting attendance—if you're supposed to bring the beverages, your sense of duty will get you out of the house even when you don't *feel* like going. And, chances are, once you've dressed, packed up the kids, and made it to the get-together, you'll be glad you did. (All moms know getting ready is the toughest part of going anywhere!)

People who sit on the sidelines judging the performance of others are always the toughest critics. They're not in the arena to see just how hard it is to play the game. Striving for one hundred percent member involvement is your greatest insurance policy against whiners and complainers.

It also provides protection against overworking any one member. Some groups have made the mistake of having only two officers. That's a disaster waiting to happen. If just one woman doesn't follow through on her commitments, everything—literally everything—falls on the shoulders of the other leader.

The woman who remains carries a heavy burden indeed. Watching her work her fingers to the bone is not a pretty picture. So guess what happens when it's time to elect new officers? No one wants the job!

So, get as many women involved as quickly as you can. Strive to make your network—however small or large—truly a team effort.

Common Purpose

Nothing unifies a team like having a specific mission to accomplish. As Mariette Holland, founder of the Holland Center for Professional Development, notes: "The team can't be created just around survival stuff. In order to be healthy, the team needs a purpose outside itself. Service projects, for example, can create common ground that otherwise wouldn't exist. It creates the basis for positive shared memories."

The National MOMS Club (see Resource 5, Chapter 15) also emphasizes the importance of service projects to build *esprit de corps*. Mary James, Founder and Chairperson, says, "service projects can be addicting. They're a great way for everyone to get to know each other while working together on a common goal. They provide a terrific opportunity to get involved in the community. There is something truly heartwarming about being able to look back at what you've accomplished and knowing you have helped someone in need."

The MOMS Club manual includes a whole chapter explaining exactly how to organize successful service projects. Some of the service projects their members have done in the past include

- Recycling aluminum cans, then donating the money to charity
- Hosting holiday parties for abused or orphaned children
- Visiting retirement homes
- Donating used clothes or toys to charity
- Holding garage sales or bake sales to raise money for a worthy cause
- Organizing fashion show fund-raisers
- Compiling a directory of services and businesses in your community for mothers and children

Another organization, the East Valley Women's Club of Mesa, Arizona, asks members to bring donated items to each monthly meeting for a local shelter for abused women. Because the group has an ongoing outreach to the shelter, they have a tremendous sense of making a real difference in hurting lives.

Form Special Interest Groups

Mary James, of the National MOMS Club, explains how their local chapters organize special activity groups: "As a club becomes larger, members will want to share their special interests outside of regular meetings and groupwide activities. For example, members with preschoolers may want to form playgroups, while those with school-aged children may want to arrange trips to the theater or museums. Activity groups are the ideal way to accommodate different interests within the club.

"When several members want to share a common interest on a regular basis, they may form an activity group. Each activity group should be open to all members, but the activity group does not depend on the participation of all members to survive. For example, some mothers may want to share their interest in cooking by holding a monthly gourmet luncheon. Other members of the club may think that cooking for fun is a contradiction in terms. By forming a Gourmet Lunch Bunch, the mothers who want to cook can do so and no pressure is put on the non-cooking mothers to join.

"The idea of forming an activity group will probably grow spontaneously from the interests of the members. The activity groups are not necessarily started by a club officer. It should be started by the mother or mothers who are interested in the activity. By encouraging them to start the group, leadership and initiative is fostered in the regular members and pressure is taken off the officers to provide 'services' for everyone else."

Just a few examples of special interest groups include:
- Gourmet Cooking Club
- Health Food Co-op
- Fitness or Walking Club
- Home School Co-op
- Arts and Crafts
- Decorating Club (help one another decorate your own homes)
- Coupon Co-op

Make Each Others' Lives Easier

"The only way you'll have someone there for you when needed is if you invest time to nurture the team before you get into the crisis mode," advises Mariette. "In other words, don't have a 'what can you do for me?' attitude. Instead, focus on what you can do for others, so their life is easier. And when their life is easier, they'll be in a better position to return the favor."

Of course, *No More Lone Ranger Moms* is filled with practical ideas for how you can help make other women's lives easier. Moms helping moms—that's what it's all about.

Take Time for Reflection

1. This chapter opened with a discussion about football. Keeping that analogy in mind, describe what kind of team player you are. (Are you even in the game . . . or are you sitting on the sidelines?)

_____

_____

_____

_____

2. Are you the kind of player you would want to have on your team? If not, list some practical ways you can become a better team player:

_____

_____

_____

3. Are you one hundred percent involved in the groups you belong to? If not, what practical steps can you take to demonstrate a stronger commitment?

_____

_____

_____

_____

4. Do you know some women who are sitting on the sidelines? Perhaps they belong to your church or mothers' group or maybe they just moved in down the street. List the name of that "spectator" along with some ideas for how you can encourage her to become an active part of your support network.

NAME	STRATEGIES TO ENCOURAGE INVOLVEMENT
_____	_____
_____	_____
_____	_____
_____	_____
_____	_____

5. Review the ideas for service projects. Make a note of any that strike your interest and feel free to think up additional ideas. Begin now to research how you might undertake these projects in your community.

_____

_____

_____

6. List some other ways your network can promote a sense of common purpose.

_____

_____

_____

7. List some activities you enjoy that might work well as the

basis for a special interest group. (Review the list included in the chapter, if you need inspiration.) Seek out other mothers who share your interest.

_____ _____

_____ _____

8. List mothers you know who are having a tough time right now. Perhaps they have a new baby or sickness in the family. Then note some practical ideas for how you can help make their lives a little easier.

NAME	TYPE OF HELP YOU CAN OFFER
_____	_____
_____	_____
_____	_____
_____	_____
_____	_____

8

Is Someone Following You?

EVERY NETWORK NEEDS a leader—even if she is only an informal one. So, what qualities does it take to effectively lead women? Of course, the requirements will vary depending upon whether you are leading three neighborhood women forming a playgroup or a church women's ministry with 50 members. In a previous chapter, we examined the four types of moms along with the strengths and weaknesses of each. Remember, no personality type is better than another. Any woman who understands her own strengths and weaknesses can be an excellent leader, even if she is naturally reserved.

More important than a leader's personality type is her heart attitude. She needs to have a "Servant's Heart." Actually, all of us would do well to cultivate these attitudes, not just those who desire to lead. We are *all* role models for other women, the only question is whether we are a good role model . . . or a poor one. So what are the characteristics of a woman with a servant's heart? Let's take a look.

Hospitality

The surest demonstration of a servant's heart is hospitality. A servant leader must be willing to host special events and meetings in her home. And she must be willing to invite other women over, for one-on-one time. People who enter her home, or attend a meeting where she presides, should feel welcome and wanted. Your home doesn't have to be spotlessly clean to invite a friend over. Your cooking doesn't have to be good enough to impress Martha Stewart. In fact, perfect homes often make people feel *unwelcome*. They are so afraid of spilling something on the spotlessly clean, white carpet, they can't relax. And a hostess who's fussing over every little detail doesn't have time to get to know her guests. So, relax! You don't have to be the perfect hostess, just a caring hostess.

Encourager

Poor leaders discourage people. They may have unrealistic expectations and make people feel inferior or guilty if they don't measure up. That's a real danger for perfectionists, like the Meticulous Mom. A leader can also discourage people by making them feel their needs and opinions don't count. That's where the Take-Charge Mom can really get into trouble, by insisting on doing things *her way*—also known as the *right way*.

Good leaders encourage people. They make others feel good about themselves and about the contribution they can make to the network. They focus on finding and bringing out the best in others. Wouldn't we all love to have more encouraging people in our lives? Why not start by being an encouragement to others? Maybe you'll start a new trend in your neighborhood or church.

Ability to Change People's Attitudes and Behaviors

The ability to help people change for the better is the most powerful and meaningful role of a true leader. In his book *How to Win Friends and Influence People* (Simon & Shuster, 1981, p. 275), Dale Carnegie shares nine principles of leadership, all designed to help change other people's attitudes and behaviors *without giving offense.*

That part about *not giving offense* is absolutely key. We are all experts on what's wrong with everyone else. We're not so fond of taking a hard look at what's wrong in our own lives. Jesus gave the best advice for dealing with this issue. "Do not judge, or you too will be judged. For in the same way you judge others, you will be judged, and with the measure you use, it will be measured to you. Why do you look at the speck of sawdust in your brother's eye and pay no attention to the plank in your own eye? How can you say to your brother, 'Let me take the speck out of your eye,' when all the time there is a plank in your own eye? You hypocrite, first take the plank out of your own eye, and then you will see clearly to remove the speck from your brother's eye" (Matthew 7:1–5). Then Jesus put it even more succinctly. "In everything, do to others what you would have them do to you" (Matthew 7:12).

In keeping with treating others the way we want to be treated, here are the nine principles of leadership advocated by Dale Carnegie:

1. Begin with praise and honest appreciation.
2. Call attention to people's mistakes indirectly.
3. Talk about your own mistakes before criticizing the other person.
4. Ask questions instead of giving direct orders.
5. Let the other person save face.
6. Praise the slightest improvement and praise every improvement.
7. Give the other person a fine reputation to live up to.
8. Use encouragement. Make the fault seem easy to correct.

9. Make the other person happy about doing the thing you suggest.

If you learn to deal with people according to those nine principles, you'll not only become a great leader, you'll be a great person and a great friend, as well.

Transparency

In order to make a difference in other people's lives, you've got to be real. That means being transparent enough for people to get to know you for who you really are. It means getting past the superficial games people play; it means letting down your guard and being vulnerable enough to let people into your life.

However, a word of warning is needed here. This transparency business can be a bit tricky. I always thought transparency was the same as airing your dirty laundry or letting people see you at your worst. I thought it meant saying whatever you thought, regardless of how your words might affect others. I prided myself on "being real" and looked down on the "phony balonies" who kept the conversation light. I was wrong and the quality of my relationships reflected just how wrong I was.

Does that mean we should be phony? That we should never say what we mean or mean what we say? Not at all. You can only keep up a good front for so long before the "real" you emerges. If you pretend to be someone you're not, it's only a matter of time before the women around you realize the truth. If you have allowed them to put you up on a pedestal, prepare for a crash landing. The very women who admired you will come to resent you.

So where's the balance? I don't know about you, but I have struggled with that question for years. I think I discovered the answer one day in my sister's living room. She has a collection of glass water balls or snow balls—they usually contain a small winter scene. One water ball features a beautiful snow princess. When you gaze through the transparent glass into her private little world, it is beautiful and captivating to behold. Even when you turn the ball upside down, even when the imaginary snow swirls all about her, she stands firm. She remains the same regardless of circumstances; she remains composed.

If your private world was surrounded by a water ball, so all the world could gaze upon you in the midst of life's storms, would it be beautiful to behold? Your heart is the key to meaningful transparency. When who you are on the inside is consistently beautiful, your life is a joy to behold. Are you the kind of woman that others desire to emulate? That is the measure of true leadership. Do you long to become that kind of woman? I know I do.

Take Time for Reflection

1. Examine your heart. Pray and reflect upon whether your core desire is to serve or be served. Note your thoughts below:

_____

_____

_____

2. When was the last time you invited a group of friends for a get-together (birthday parties don't count!) in your home?

_____

3. Plan now to host an informal gathering.
DATE: _____
TIME: _____
OCCASION OR THEME (fun, but not required): _____

LIST OF INVITED GUESTS:

_____   _____

_____   _____

_____   _____

_____   _____

4. When was the last time you spent time, one-on-one, with someone who was new in your life (i.e., new in the

neighborhood or new to your church, rather than your usual friends)?_____

5. List someone you will invite over:_____
When?_____

6. In general, how hospitable are you? Rate yourself on a scale of 1 to 10, with 10 being the most hospitable:

          1 2 3 4 5 6 7 8 9 10

7. Make a list of all the people who make you feel good about being you:

_____   _____

_____   _____

_____   _____

_____   _____

_____   _____

NOTE: I gave you plenty of room, hoping you have plenty of encouraging people in your life. If not, seek them out. You can never get enough encouragement.

8. How do you feel about the people you listed—the people who make you feel good about being you?_____

(The point is, of course, it's hard not to like such people. In the same way, if you make others feel good about themselves, they'll feel good about you.)

9. List five friends and, for each, list a specific way you can make them feel good about who they are—now, or in the future. Perhaps you can buy them a gift the next time you're on vacation, or write them a note expressing appreciation, or take them out to lunch, etc.

FRIEND	WAYS TO MAKE HER FEEL GOOD ABOUT HERSELF
_____	_____
_____	_____
_____	_____
_____	_____
_____	_____

10. Rate your leadership (or role model) quotient based on the nine principles of leadership set forth by Dale Carnegie:

PRINCIPLE	ALWAYS	SOME-TIMES	NEVER
• When you want to help someone change a negative habit or attitude, do you begin with praise and honest appreciation?	☐	☐	☐
• Do you call attention to people's mistakes indirectly?	☐	☐	☐
• Do you talk about your own mistakes before criticizing the other person?	☐	☐	☐
• Do you ask questions instead of giving direct orders?	☐	☐	☐
• Do you let the other person save face?	☐	☐	☐
• Are you sure to praise the slightest improvement?	☐	☐	☐
• Do you give the other person a fine reputation to live up to?	☐	☐	☐
• Do you rely on encouragement to promote change? Do you make the fault seem easy to correct?	☐	☐	☐

- Do you help the other person feel   ☐   ☐   ☐
  good about doing what you sug-
  gest?

NOTE: The ultimate leader will respond "Always" to all nine principles. The rest of us mere mortals will have to settle for less! On the other hand, if you circled "Never" for most items, you should not yet seek a position of leadership in your church or your community.

11. Which principle will you begin cultivating in your life—starting today? _____

PART THREE

THE REALITY

9
Building Your Own Support Network

MOTHERHOOD IS A WONDERFUL EQUALIZER. Whether you are trained as a brain surgeon or a receptionist, if your child refuses to toilet train you've got the same problem on your hands. When your teenager turns into a tyrant, you're in the same boat with world-renowned physicists. That's the beauty of a mothers' support network. It's a place where women can find common ground and help each other deal with the common problems of mothering. It doesn't matter if you're the mother of a preschooler or the parent of teenagers, you still need the support of other mothers. So, let's get down to the nuts-and-bolts of organizing a mothers' support network.

Two Main Types of Support Groups

Before we proceed, however, we need to distinguish between playgroups and co-ops. What's the difference? The primary objective of a playgroup is for the children to have opportunity to play and/or for moms to have a chance to socialize.

In contrast, a co-op seeks to give the mother an opportunity to "take a break" from her everyday responsibilities or to devote herself to projects which can be handled more efficiently if she focuses her attention. Co-op members are more interested in supporting one another in very practical ways, such as described in this section.

You'll probably detect my own bias toward co-ops on the pages of this book, although we'll also provide a lot of information on playgroups. Don't misunderstand. I think talking about motherhood and watching your child interact with others are both very valuable activities. But in today's hectic society, many mothers need more than talking. They need help. And for women who watch their children all day long, the opportunity to *not* watch their children for an hour or so is a welcomed respite. She may need to run to the grocery store quickly. (And, let's be honest: children, grocery store, and *quickly* are a pretty rare combination!) Perhaps she needs a haircut, or time to devote to a special project. Maybe she runs a home business, and the co-op takes the place of daycare. In short, playgroups are for playing and socializing. Co-ops are for working and helping.

You will need to make it clear from day one which kind of network you plan to be: a playgroup or a co-op. You may decide to begin as a playgroup. And as friendships begin to blossom, as trust begins to form, and as you become aware of one another's needs, you may begin gradually adding more of the practical activities described here. Or perhaps you're already part of MOPS or a ladies' Bible study, and several of the members would like to develop a playgroup or co-op. In either case, the first step is to define your needs.

Defining Your Needs

It's very important to be clear about what you need. Are you looking to find playmates for your child or friends for yourself? Maybe a little of both? Do you simply want to watch your child play and interact with others? Or do you need practical help as a mother? Things like babysitting, cooking, and exchanging baby clothes. Do you need someone to make a meal when you bring home a new baby? Once you've determined what you need, you can decide whether a playgroup or a co-op is right for you.

How Large Will the Network Be?

You also need to decide on a specific limit to the number of participants. At what point will you branch off and start new groups? On what basis will you divide? You can divide by geography. Women may become more active in the co-op if the other members are very close to home. You can divide by age. One common approach is by birth year, so that all women with children born in 1990 would form a network, 1991 would form another, etc. The tricky part is what to do about women with more than one child. You can leave it to the mother's discretion. She can join more than one network, or you can establish a rule that she must join the network associated with her eldest child, or the youngest. Whatever works best for your network is fine. The important thing is to make it clear up front exactly how you will handle this. If it seems arbitrary (or worse, based on personalities, favoritism, and cliques), conflict is sure to erupt. Remember: An ounce of prevention is worth a pound of cure.

There are some well-established groups, such as Las Madres in California, that have been in existence for many years. Their membership is constantly growing and evolving. Yet, the individual sub-groups are always limited in size. Most experienced mothers agree that five to seven women is the ideal size for a playgroup. Co-ops can be much larger.

The Golden Rule

As I have talked with women from around the country who have participated in mothers' support groups, I wanted to discover "The Golden Rule" for success. My initial assumptions were: bigger is better and the more organized the better. And, yes, there are large and very successful groups. And, yes, they are all extremely well organized. But I have also discovered that many extremely small groups (three to five women) are also effective in meeting the needs of their members.

I have heard about many groups that have failed, almost all of which were small to mid-sized (six to fifteen). In trying to determine why some support networks are tremendously effective while others fall flat, here's the golden rule I've hit upon:

> If you want a small support network, the members had better *really like* each other and be radically committed to sticking together through thick and thin. If you want to build a mid-size to large network, you had better be extremely organized and clear about what's what and who's who. Groups that do not fall into one of these two categories—small and committed or large and organized—are virtually doomed to failure.

New Moms and Old

Another factor to consider is whether you want to restrict your network to first-time mothers only, experienced mothers only, or go for a combination of both. Do you want all of the women in your network to have school-aged children, because that's where you're at? Our network welcomes all mothers, however, "many [groups] consist exclusively of new mothers; they fulfill an important need. It is a great forum in which to talk about new teeth, toilet training, bottles, and such with other women who are going through these developments at the same time," says Jody Gaylin, writing for *Parents Magazine.* "But once you've been through all of these with one or two children, it is wonderful to meet with a group and talk about other things."

Our local church has a support group just for parents of teenagers—maybe you'd like to form a "Mothers of Teenagers" (aka The MOTley Crew!). On the other hand, there's something to be said for the older woman teaching the younger. There's something wonderfully fulfilling about giving back and sharing what you've learned. And there's something very comforting in hearing that you're not the first mother to go through these trials and you will make it through. Even better is to hear, "I remember what it's like . . . how can I help you?" Unfortunately, those words are not uttered nearly enough by experienced moms.

Finding a Founding Partner

You can try to launch a mothers' network on your own, but your chances of success are doubled if you find a partner who shares your enthusiasm. In addition to dividing the work, you can encourage each other during the early days when the going may be tough. Expect the planning stage to take one to two months if you undertake the project alone. You should be off and running much faster with a little help from a friend.

Another important factor is cost. Before you have dues-paying members, you'll need to print up Membership Packets including laminated half-hour cards, Rules and Regulations, Emergency Authorization Cards, Membership Profile forms, roster sheets, and more. (You will find samples of these tools in Chapter 15.) You'll probably want to put the information in attractive folders with the name of your mothers' support network on the front. Add the refreshments needed for your first organizational meeting, and you can see how all of this can really add up. Hopefully, your partner or partners can split the cost with you. (NOTE: Keep careful track of your expenses. Once you recruit members, you can use their dues to reimburse yourself.)

What to Look for in a Partner

Your natural inclination may be to choose someone . . . just like you. Wrong approach! What's needed is someone who isn't like you. If you are detail oriented and good with planning and organization, then you need a creative, outgoing partner. If you're a great idea person who gets all excited about new projects, you'll play a very important role in the success of the support network. But you had better join forces with someone who specializes in finishing projects and handling all the "boring" details involved.

The most important qualification for a founding partner is someone with a positive, can-do attitude. And someone with a proven track record for getting things done. The world is filled with eager-beaver starters; what you need is a steady finisher.

Recruiting Members

The first challenge in forming your new mothers' support network also happens to be one of the toughest: finding members. Fortunately, ingenious mothers have successfully tried dozens of techniques. If you are look-ing for three other moms for a playgroup, you can probably skip the following section. But if you want to launch a babysitting co-op or a large playgroup, read on:

Flyers

A very affordable approach is to create your own promotional flyer and distribute it yourself. Many office supply stores and print shops make copies for three to six cents apiece. So you can reach hundreds of women for less than $10. If you have access to a computer or typewriter, that will give your flyer a more professional look. If not, handwritten will do. Remember to make your flyer attractive and creative. You want it to be a positive reflection of the group's potential.

The key is to always keep a supply of the flyers available: at home, in your car, in the diaper bag, in your purse. That way, if you meet a woman you think might be a good candidate for your network, give her a flyer and invite her to attend your first (or next) event.

Business Cards

If the prospect of carting around flyers seems too difficult, you can have business cards printed up with the basic information about your co-op. For around $15, you can print 500 cards. That's probably enough to last through your grandchildren's lifetime. These can be posted on bulletin boards in grocery stores, libraries, churches, YWCAs, etc. And, of course, they are easy enough to carry to the park or wherever else you might run across a prospective member. If your goal is to grow a large support network—one that will eventually divide into many smaller sub-groups—you should definitely have business cards printed. Give an ample supply to each new member and constantly encourage them to spread the news. Handing someone a business card is a very low-pressure approach to that end.

Press Releases

A press release is a notice sent to local newspapers with information about your network. You can use wording similar to the sample press release provided in Chapter 15. The newspaper does not charge to run your release; such information is carried as a service to the community. Of course, since you are not paying for the publicity (as you would if you placed an advertisement) there is no guarantee that the newspaper will run it. Nor do you control when they will run it. It's at their sole discretion, but chances are very good you will get coverage in your local newspaper. That's important, because people who don't read the Classified Ads may notice the announcement. When the founders of the co-op I belong to sent a two-paragraph release to the local newspaper, they heard from more than twenty prospective members.

Again, if growth is part of your plan, you can continue to seek publicity on a regular—even monthly—basis. Notify the media of any special events you sponsor, such as a guest speaker or any special events that are open to the public. You can also take photos (black and white preferred) of your more interesting activities and send them out along with a press release. This is the ideal way to keep your co-op in the news and foremost on the minds of new moms. For example, we sent photographs of our Easter Egg Hunt to the local paper and landed on the front page.

Not everyone will set out to launch a giant, statewide mothers' support network. But once you see what it can do for mothers, chances are you—and other members—will want to share the good news. This is a powerful, life-changing solution to the dilemma facing most mothers. Let's get the word out!

Word of Mouth

Most playgroups and co-ops begin by simple word of mouth—often called the most effective advertising strategy in the world. You tell two friends you're starting a network, they each tell two friends, and pretty soon you've got a solid core of members. If your goal is just to join forces with a few moms in your church or neighborhood, this approach may be all you need. It also gives you more control over who joins the network. For example, you may want only mothers from your neighborhood or church. Also, when everyone is invited by a friend of a friend, your chances of forming a compatible group are improved. We formed a support group for home-schooling moms, using this strategy. Six women showed up for the first meeting! We had so much fun, our one-hour meeting lasted four hours!

Open House

This is how one group I belong to, Red Mountain Ranch Mothers' Co-op, was formed. In addition to a notice in the newspaper, Cindi Lester and Anita Wingfield posted signs around the neighborhood inviting any interested moms to attend an Open House at Cindi's house. Fourteen women showed up that first night, and most immediately became members. Of course, there's always some risk involved when you open your home to the public. You may want to make the event "by invitation only" and simply mail invitations to selected women. Either way—open to the public or by invitation—an Open House is a great way to jump-start your network on a positive note.

Church

If you are an active member of a local church, why not ask the church secretary to put a notice in the Sunday bulletin? You can also post flyers around the church facilities and ask the head of the women's ministry to announce it, as well. Again, this is a good way to ensure that the members you attract to your network share many of the same values and priorities.

Childbirth or Parenting Class

Don't overlook these classes as a great place to recruit new members. Perhaps the sponsors will allow you to post flyers or you can ask them to announce it to their class. In fact, many support networks grow quite naturally out of the relationships formed in these classes.

Take Time for Reflection

1. Evaluate whether you want a co-op or playgroup.

If you:	Then you want a:
Just want someone for your children to play with.	Playgroup
Want to socialize with the other moms.	Playgroup
Already have a strong support network.	Playgroup
Need practical help caring for your children.	Co-op
Are willing to provide help to other moms.	Co-op
Want someone to make a meal when you're sick, etc.	Co-op
Are willing to make a meal for other moms.	Co-op
Want to exchange babysitting services.	Co-op

2. Ideally, how large would you like your network to be?

_____

3. Will you include only new moms, experienced moms, or both?_____

4. Will your network be moms only, or will you include baby-sitters and other childcare providers?_____

5. Evaluate your strengths and weaknesses for starting a moms' support network.

Strengths	Weaknesses
_____	_____
_____	_____
_____	_____

6. Based on your evaluation, describe your ideal founding partner:

_____

_____

_____

7. List everyone who might help you launch your mothers' support network.

_____	_____
_____	_____
_____	_____

8. Which of the following strategies will you use to promote the network?

	Will Use (√)	Completed (√)
Flyers	_____	_____
Business Cards	_____	_____
Press Releases	_____	_____
Word of mouth	_____	_____
Church	_____	_____
Childbirth class	_____	_____
Parenting class	_____	_____

NOTE: See Chapter 15 for samples of promotional material you can use.

10
How to Start a Playgroup

THERE ARE TWO DISTINCT types of playgroups, each with very different objectives. Before you launch headlong into the playgroup adventure, you should evaluate which style meets your needs.

The first playgroup form is Unstructured Playgroup and the emphasis is on shared experiences. Such groups typically meet weekly, and often at the same location every time. For example, a community center, park, or church facility. All mothers and their children attend every week. Usually, the groups include seven to eight mothers and their children. Although there certainly is room for variation, the groups tend to promote unstructured play while the mothers get to know one another.

The second form, Structured Playgroup or Sit and Play, involves rotating leadership among participating mothers. Once per week, all of the children gather at one home. It should be limited to four mothers, with no more than six children altogether. The mother who hosts plans the activities and provides refreshments for everyone. The playgroup time should be well prepared in advance, with time for structured learning. The other mothers are free to pursue other interests or responsibilities for two and a half to three hours. (Their turn will come around soon enough!)

Neither form is necessarily better than the other; it

just depends on what you hope to accomplish. If you are looking for a substitute for institutional child care—such as a nursery or preschool, the Structured Playgroup provides learning opportunities, free time for you, and is virtually free.

If your real goal is to get to know other mothers while providing your child with an opportunity to play with other children, you should opt to join (or form your own) Unstructured Playgroup.

If you are not completely sure which type to choose, you may want to begin with the Unstructured Playgroup, so you can get to know the other mothers and their children. Once you have a better idea of who's who, you can invite a smaller number to become part of a Structured Playgroup.

Unstructured Playgroups

If your child is under three, you'll want to take a more unstructured approach to your playgroup. In fact, many moms with older children find that an unstructured playgroup meets their needs just fine—with a lot less work than the structured variety.

As with any playgroup, the age of the children involved is a key factor. "Enterprising mothers who have a wide variety of age-appropriate toys on hand might find that mixing two-year-olds with four-year-olds is no problem, but for the most part, too big an age difference, and the group doesn't have a chance," says Jody Gaylin, writing for *Parents Magazine* (January 1988, p. 73).

Once again, the ideal arrangement is to divide the children by birth year. It's much easier for the children to play together, the mothers have more in common and can learn more by observing one another's children. Also, mothers have different objectives depending upon their child's age. For example "a six-month-old's mother is there to meet other mothers, whereas the mother of a toddler is there to encourage her child to learn to socialize and share," says Gaylin.

Where to Have Playgroup

You can elect to hold your playgroup in the members' homes on a rotating basis, or one mom who has an exceptionally large playroom may be willing to serve as permanent host. In that case, she should be exempted from ever providing refreshments! However, many unstructured playgroups prefer meeting outside the home—in parks, recreation centers, or churches. That's because the free-style approach results in, well, a mess!

"When our children were still babies, we alternated houses, serving coffee for moms and a snack for kids. Because the kids were young, we could control where they ate, so the mess was confined to kitchen or dining room and everyone was relaxed. You don't need an enormous space for small children," says Gaylin. "Once our kids got older and more mobile and active, we quickly moved to the local community center, which provided both free space and toys. It became too trying, even for the least compulsive among us, to watch six children drop crackers all over the living room and then grind them into the rug," recalls Gaylin. "Now it is great not to have to clean house. We still bring coffee and snacks. We were worried, at first, about the loss of intimacy in such a large room. But we've found that the enormous space, with its riding toys, a tunnel, a slide, and a lot of blocks and books, means that the children spend time away from our laps, leaving us relatively free to talk."

Field Trips

Following is just a sampling of no-cost and low-cost field trips for preschoolers and their moms. Also, check out the excellent book, *The Yellow Pages Guide to Edu-*

cational Field Trips, by Greg Harris (1–800–225–5259).

- Beach Day—Bring shovels, buckets, funnels, and empty milk cartons for building sand castles.
- Candy Shop—Let the children see how their favorites are made . . . but don't let them test too much of the merchandise.
- Dairy Farm—A local dairy farm recently gave our co-op children a delightful tour.
- Nature Walk—Go to the nearest park, forest, or recreation area. Look for branches, leaves, flowers, stones, pine cones, and other items you can use to create special treasures.
- Puppet shows—Our co-op recently attended a puppet show version of the *Three Billy Goats Gruff*. It was held FREE at the local library.
- Zoo—It's hard to go wrong at the zoo. Kids love it!
- Fire Station—Here's another free activity that our co-op children enjoyed. All that's needed is a phone call to the local fire station; they are only too happy to oblige.
- Small Airport—We did this one, too! The children really enjoyed getting a close-up view of the airplanes taking off and landing. And because the planes are smaller, the children feel more at home than they do around the giant planes at major airports.
- Library or Children's bookstore—Most libraries and many of the larger bookstores have regular reading hours. It's fun and free.
- Your imagination is the limit!

The Benefits of Structured Playgroups

Ann Hoyer, of Sanford, North Carolina, says: "I figured at least I'd gain free time and a guaranteed nap on playgroup days by joining a playgroup, but since Jed was my first child I didn't realize how much more than that I'd get. Planning a morning for the children turned out to be interesting and entertaining. Very soon I realized that young preschoolers accomplish much more than I'd expected. It became challenging to see what new ideas would catch the children's attention. It was surprising how quickly the kids could run through what I thought was a full-morning program. Another surprise was how quickly they could run through what looked like an inexhaustible supply of apple juice.

"Playgroup helped me to see other children Jed's age at close range regularly. Their company behavior wore off, and as I watched their everyday personalities at work together, I developed a more realistic perspective on Jed's behavior. It was a relief to see that other children sulked and balked. Of course, knowing the other children meant conceding there could be other children as precocious and adorable as my Jed. I do believe that the time spent with other toddlers helped me deal with Jed more reasonably.

"As a newcomer in town, playgroup was a good chance for me to become close to other parents, parents who by choosing to do a playgroup stood out as concerned and generous in spirit. It was helpful to have these friends during those parenting crisis times. When I went to them with a problem about Jed I knew I was getting the opinion of parents who had worked with my child over many weeks. They had seen him laughing, screaming, spilling, pinching, coping, and not coping. Their helpful listening, discussing, and advice were super indeed."*

Keys to a Successful Structured Playgroup

It takes quite a bit of effort and mutual trust to conduct a successful Structured Playgroup. Through trial and error, the pioneers of the playgroup movement have

---

*Reprinted from *Come With Us to Playgroup*, by Patricia Boggia Magee and Marilyn Reichwald Ornstein, Prentice-Hall, 1981.

discovered some do's and don'ts you should keep in mind.

Limit the Number of Children

According to the experts—including moms and teachers—the ideal number of children that one adult can handle effectively is five. As soon as the group grows beyond that number, the mother can't give the proper amount of attention to each individual child. And you know what happens when children don't get the attention they need, right? Mayhem!

Some playgroups allow as many as seven children per mother, which is workable if you do not expect to teach the children very much. If the group really is strictly for playing, you might be able to stretch it that far. But be forewarned, it won't be easy.

One way to expand the number of children involved, without going completely out of your mind, is for two mothers to conduct the playgroup together. In that case, you can handle ten children, providing you have the facilities to do so. For example, it would be just fine in a church nursery or community center. Ten children would be pretty tough to handle in a private home during a snowstorm. Use your own good judgment.

What you want to avoid is a worst-case-daycare-scenario, where children are left to entertain and fend for themselves. The mothers who will want to join your playgroup are women who have chosen to stay at home, often at great sacrifice, because they believe in the importance of nurturing children. If your playgroup contradicts their basic values, your playgroup members won't stay around very long.

Restrict Age Range of Children

The ideal playgroup consists of children born within the same year. If you have hundreds of members, like

Las Madres, you can arrange the best of all possible playgroups. The rest of us will have to do the best we can. It goes without saying that the closer in age the better. The real problems arise when you try to mingle crawling babies with three-year-olds . . . especially boys. Can't you just see a three-year-old at the wheel of a Little Tikes mobile, closing in on a hapless six-month-old at half-a-room per minute?!

Choose the Right Playgroup Members

Choosing the right members is the key to a successful playgroup. Be sure to choose carefully. *Come With Us to Playgroup* (quoted above) includes a checklist of the qualities that make a mom a good playgroup participant:

1. Does the mother appear relaxed with her own child?
2. Does the mother seem to enjoy interacting with young children?
3. In discussions about various things that can be done with young children, does the mother seem responsive and interested in carrying out these activities?
4. Does the mother exhibit a sense of humor about the antics of young children?
5. Does the mother seem patient and understanding with her own child?
6. When the child speaks to the mother, does she truly listen and respond?
7. When discipline is necessary, does the mother avoid the issue or deal directly with it? Does this involve screaming across the room or approaching the child and dealing with the situation face to face and with understanding?
8. Is a warm, friendly greeting part of the mother's approach to your child in casual meetings?
9. How does the mother react to minor spills and accidents?
10. Do you feel comfortable talking with the mother?

Have you some things in common (older siblings, interests, age, profession)? (Boggia, pp. 16–17)

I must confess, if you were checking me out, I would probably flunk the test. So don't be too critical. Nevertheless, the above guidelines are helpful. Never recruit a new member hastily. Remember, you are dealing with the care of your most precious possession, so this is nothing to rush into. Take time to observe the other mother in action. Invite her over for lunch, go to the park together and find out if she shares your core values and priorities as a parent. Otherwise, trouble looms ahead.

Set Objectives

Prior to your first playgroup session, all the mothers should sit down and discuss their objectives. What do you hope to achieve? Why are you joining together? What expectations do you have of the other mothers when it's their turn to lead the group?

Is it enough for the children to play and have fun? Or do you expect them to learn something new? Do you envision a preschool environment with structured lessons? How much time should the hosting mom devote to story time, learning time, and crafts, etc.? When you sit down at the table, don't expect everyone to be in complete agreement. However, by the time your first meeting is over, you should have a written list of playgroup objectives that everyone can agree upon. Each mom may have to compromise a little, but that's all part of it.

This initial meeting will go a long way toward insuring the long-term success of your playgroup.

Establish Guidelines

Once you have a clear set of objectives that all the moms agree to, next you need to establish guidelines.

Some issues you'll want to address include:

1. How much preparation time should the mothers invest when it's their time to lead?
2. What type of snacks will be provided? Are some food and drink items off limits (i.e., soda and junk food)?
3. Will all mothers be expected to adhere to a particular schedule?
4. Will you share resources (like paints, glue, glitter, fabric scraps, etc.)? Or will each mother provide her own resources when it's her turn?
5. Will you share expenses? Or will each mom pay for the activities she chooses?
6. If you decide to share resources, will you assign a coordinator to store and dispense supplies as needed?

Share Responsibility

At the heart of the Structured Playgroup is an emphasis on shared responsibility. Each of the mothers commits herself to providing a fun, enriching experience for everyone's children when it's her turn to lead. If one member fails to prepare, either occasionally or consistently, she is not only letting the other mothers down, she is also shortchanging the children.

Again, before beginning the playgroup, the mothers need to clarify their expectations for one another. Do you expect the moms to invest thirty minutes to throw together the day's activities? Or do you expect hours of work and planning? If one mother pulls out all the stops, while another pulls out the VCR, resentment is bound to grow.

One way to guard against dashed expectations is to spell out, in writing, exactly what is expected of each other. It also helps to provide a basic playgroup format that each mother should follow. This consistency of routine is also good for the children. Since they'll be rotating locations each week, they will find comfort in the sameness of the activities. (NOTE: That's not to say that each mom can't have a unique specialty. One mom may specialize in fun art projects, another might emphasize music, and still another, drama.) The schedule for a two-hour playgroup might be organized as follows:

Playgroup Schedule

9:00—9:30	Free Play
9:30—10:00	Planned Activity (handicraft, finger plays)
10:00—10:30	Snack Time with Story (mom may read, recite, dramatize, or play an audiotape)
10:30—11:00	Physical Activity (music, games, outdoor play)

You can also provide each mother with a playgroup preparation checklist, such as the one that follows.

If you can't count on the other mothers to carry their weight, the playgroup will simply become a source of frustration for you. Use encouragement to promote everyone's best effort. Encourage friendly competition and let each of the mom's try to outdo each other in planning a great time for the children. (Careful, though!)

Playgroup Preparation Checklist

1. Materials Needed for Free Play:
   - ☐ _____
   - ☐ _____
   - ☐ _____
2. Planned Activity Description:
   - ☐ _____
3. Supplies Needed for Planned Activity:
   - ☐ _____
   - ☐ _____

☐ _____
☐ _____

4. Snacks:
   ☐ _____
   ☐ _____
   ☐ _____

5. Snack-time Story:
   ☐ _____

6. Physical Activities Planned:
   ☐ _____
   ☐ _____

7. Supplies needed for Physical Activities:
   ☐ _____
   ☐ _____
   ☐ _____
   ☐ _____

OTHER ITEMS:
   ☐ Juice
   ☐ Paper cups
   ☐ Paper plates
   ☐ Napkins

Divide the Work

In order for your Sit and Play to succeed, it's important to divide the work fairly. The simplest approach is for each mother to take full responsibility for planning the program when her turn rolls around. You can certainly choose that option. However, pooling your resources has many advantages, including:

- Cost savings by buying in bulk
- Access to more materials
- Consistent quality of instruction
- Consistent quality of activities and materials

These advantages are especially helpful if your network grows large enough to divide into several Playgroups who opt to share resources.

Supply Coordinator

Rather than each mother purchasing and storing her own supplies, you can assign one mother (who has a lot of extra storage space) to keep track of the supplies. The Supply Coordinator could be responsible for buying, storing, and dispensing materials. All materials would be purchased and used cooperatively.

The Supply Coordinator position could rotate every so often, perhaps four times per year: January, April, July, and October. Here are some supplies you should eventually have on hand. (Don't expect to gather all of these items for the first day.) Check off each item as it becomes available.

Suggested Supplies

ART SUPPLIES

- ☐ Paint
- ☐ Paintbrushes
- ☐ Play-Doh
- ☐ Homemade clay
- ☐ Magic markers
- ☐ Crayons
- ☐ Construction paper
- ☐ Glue
- ☐ Scissors (child-safe)

DRAMATIC PLAY

- ☐ Dress-up clothes
- ☐ Props
- ☐ Dolls
- ☐ Cardboard house
- ☐ Cardboard refrigerator

EDUCATIONAL MATERIALS

- ☐ Books
- ☐ Puppets
- ☐ Flannel board
- ☐ Flannel shapes
- ☐ Timeline*
- ☐ Audio Memory Publishing*

HOUSEHOLD ITEMS

- ☐ Egg cartons
- ☐ Milk cartons
- ☐ Milk jugs
- ☐ Orange juice cans
- ☐ Toilet paper rolls
- ☐ Paper towel rolls
- ☐ Paper plates
- ☐ Empty spice bottles
- ☐ Old greeting cards
- ☐ Margarine containers
- ☐ Yogurt containers

MUSIC

- ☐ Audio cassette player
- ☐ Cassette tapes
- ☐ Instruments

SPIRITUAL GROWTH

- ☐ Beginning the Walk*
- ☐ Konos Curriculum*
- ☐ Konos Timeline*
- ☐ Memlock*

STORAGE BINS

- ☐ Various size for storing play materials

TOYS

- ☐ Blocks
- ☐ Legos
- ☐ Shape sorters
- ☐ Color games
- ☐ Card games

*See Recommended Materials

Recommended Materials

AUDIO MEMORY PUBLISHING
2060 Raymond Avenue
Signal Hill, CA 90806
1–800–365-SING

This company's slogan is "You never forget what you sing." They may very well be right. In less than a week, my four-year-old daughter could name every state in the U.S. in geographic order. And she made it a point to play the tape for everyone—child or adult—who entered our home for the next several weeks. Audio Memory has a range of audio cassette tapes including Grammar Songs, Geography Songs, Math Songs, and others. Kids love them . . . and so do parents!

KONOS, INC.
P.O. Box 1534
Richardson, TX 75080
(214) 669–8337

Konos Curriculum, Volume 1
If the children in your group are four years of age and older, and you would like to do some quality teaching, investigate the Konos Curriculum. Volume 1 can be used to home school children from Pre-K through sixth grade. It is filled with fun, hands-on, Bible-based learn-

ing activities which you could easily adapt to a weekly Playgroups. If you are thinking about home schooling— especially cooperative home schooling—this is a great way to test the waters.

Konos Kids' Timeline

This companion to Konos Curriculum, Volume 1, includes a colorful, laminated timeline from A.D. 2000 to the present, along with laminated characters to post at the appropriate place in history as you learn about them. You can also obtain the Timeline only (no characters).

MEMLOCK
420 E. Montwood Avenue
LaHabra, CA 90631
1–800–373–1947

A fun, simple system for memorizing Scripture that even three-year-olds can master. The system includes 700 Bible verses divided into 48 different topics. Thanks to the memorable (well, downright silly) pictures associated with each verse, children can easily memorize one verse per week. The creator, Drake Mariani, grants permission for your co-op or playgroup to share one Memlock set. You can make enlarged photocopies of the memory cards for the children to color. A great investment!

PRODUCTS WITH A PURPOSE
Box 20885
Phoenix, AZ 85046–0885
(602) 482–8440

Beginning the Walk

This delightful book, and its companion scrapbook, are a wonderful way to develop your preschooler's faith. Each lesson includes Bible verses, suggested lesson dialogue, and simple hands-on activities, appropriate for children three and up. My daughter begs me for her daily Bible time. You can purchase one Teacher's Manual to share, and a scrapbook for each child.

GREAT CHRISTIAN BOOKS
229 S. Bridge Street
P.O. Box 8000
Elkton, MD 21922–8000
1–800–775–5422

This mail-order catalog has got it all—hundreds of books, tapes, games, and other fun stuff for teaching little ones (big ones, too!). Most items are offered at sharp discounts. Call and ask for their home education catalog. It's one of the best single source catalogs for home-based education.

HOME SCHOOL FAVORITES CATALOG
P.O. Box 2250
Gresham, OR 97030
1–800–225–5259

Perhaps you don't have time to sort through giant catalogs. Or maybe you're not quite sure what you're looking for. If you want the inside track on which home education items are the best of the best, then this catalog is for you. Each item is hand-picked by well-known home-education expert Gregg Harris.

THE TIMBERDOODLE
E1510 Spencer Lake Road
Shelton, WA 98584
(206) 426–0672

The Timberdoodle is a delightful blend of a magazine, a mail-order catalog, and a "consumer reports" of home education. You can order everything from Legos and Koosh Balls to delightful Artpacs, colored pencils, and fun stickers. You'll also find kid's gardening kits, cuisinaire rods, puzzles, and, of course, plenty of great books.

Supplies From the Community

Your neighborhood is filled with FREE STUFF that can be transformed into great material for child's play.

Cartons. If you have the space, excellent playhouses can be constructed from the cartons in which refrigerators are sold. Ask your local appliance store to save you one or watch for new neighbors on your block. Windows and a door can be easily cut, curtains put on the windows, and you have a very inexpensive indoor playhouse. Hand the children paints or markers and let them decorate the house inside and out.

Film Containers. The little plastic containers in which rolls of 35mm film are packaged can be acquired through your local photographic supply store. (Not to mention friends and relatives.) You can also ask any amateur photographer to save the containers for you. They are useful for gluing three-dimensional designs. Or how about filling them with rice, beans, or pebbles to make excellent shakers for a rhythm band or an experiment with sound.

Styrofoam Chips and Packing Pieces. There are several places where these items can be found, although securing them might require a little more scrounging on your part. Often stores receive equipment of one sort or another (medical, tools, audio) packed in large amounts of Styrofoam. It is all tossed out! The smaller Styrofoam "squiggles" can be used for stringing necklaces as well as gluing pictures. The larger Styrofoam pieces are often interesting shapes that lend themselves to building castle-like structures for small toy people, furniture, and cars. Just hand a few of these Styrofoam shapes to children and watch what they become. They are certainly more inventive play pieces than store-bought castles or houses, and you can't beat the cost!

Wallpaper Books. Any paint or home decorating store has books that are used by the customers to select wallpaper. However, when patterns of paper change and the companies issue new books, the store manager no longer needs the old books. Ask your local dealers to keep you in mind the next time a pattern change occurs. Once you have obtained a book or two, you will find they are excellent for cutting and pasting activities, as well as discussions of color and texture.

Yarn and fabric. Many projects and art activities require yarn or fabric. Of course, these items can be purchased at any craft store in your neighborhood, but this is likely to be costly. And you can easily obtain yarn and fabric from friends and relatives who sew and knit. A simple request to them about saving fabric pieces and yarn scraps will yield you a year's supply of materials.

More Ideas. For specific suggestions on fun things to do with all this material you've gathered, read *Come With Us to Playgroup: A handbook for parents and teachers of young children*, by Patricia Boggia Magee and Marilyn Reichwald Ornstein. It is jam-packed with great ideas—most of which are delightfully easy to prepare and do.

Books Worth Checking Out

Following is a list of arts and crafts books that rely on recycled or inexpensive household items. I have used them successfully with my daughter and her playmates:

SHINING STAR PUBLICATIONS
1204 Buchanan Street, Box 299
Carthage, IL 62321

Shining Star publishes the Christian Crafts Series. At

last count, they had a dozen books such as *Christian Crafts from Paper Plates* and *Christian Crafts from Egg Cartons*. They also have books on paper bag puppets, eggs, yarn art, cardboard containers, and construction paper. All good stuff.

The Make Something Club, by Frances Zweifel, NY: Puffin Books, 1994.

This book features adorable, full-color illustrations and simple instructions for a different project to make each month of the year. Suitable for even very young children. Wonderful!

Every Day in Every Way, by Cynthia Hallay and Faraday Burditt, Carthage, Ill.: Fearon Teachers' Aids, 1989.

This book is acutally a year-round calendar of preschool learning. For every weekday it includes activities (i.e., "Thinking and Talking," "Learning by Doing," "Crafts and Creations," "Songs and Games") plus "Recommended Resources." I love it!

NOTE: If you are considering home school, starting a structured playgroup is about the best preparation you could hope for.

11

How to Organize a Babysitting Co-op

THIS CHAPTER IS INCLUDED for the benefit of those readers who wish to exchange babysitting services with other mothers. **PLEASE DO NOT BE INTIMIDATED BY THE CHALLENGE OF ORGANIZING A FULL-FLEDGED BABYSITTING CO-OP.** Not everyone wants to or needs to form such a group. As with everything else included in *No More Lone Ranger Moms*, just take what you need. The following guidelines will help you keep conflicts and headaches to a minimum.

Secretarial vs. Coupon System

The first decision you'll have to make is whether your babysitting co-op will use the secretarial or coupon system for tracking hours. Our co-op uses a coupon system, so that's what is described in the sample Rules and Regulations in Chapter 15. However, please be aware that many well-established co-ops, such as Las Madres, use the secretarial system. Both have advantages and disadvantages. So let's take a quick look at both.

Secretarial System

With a secretarial system, one member maintains a central record of everyone's sitting and gadding activity.

When someone needs a sitter, she calls the acting secretary and notifies her of the date and time. The secretary then refers to her records to determine which member has the most deficit hours. (That simply means she has gadded—or dropped her children off for babysitting—more often than she has made herself available for babysitting.) The secretary then contacts the member and arranges the sit. If the member is unavailable, the secretary calls the member who has the second-most deficit hours.

At the end of babysitting, the sitter calls the secretary to report how many hours she babysat. Some groups also give additional points if a meal is served to the children, in which case, she would report that as well.

As you can see, the secretarial system involves quite a bit of bookkeeping. It also involves several phone calls back and forth every time someone needs a sitter. Another problem with this approach is, as with any group, some mothers simply don't get along. Or their children may be in conflict, or there may be a thousand different reasons why certain members prefer not to use other members. It can become very awkward for members to say, "I don't want my child with so-and-so." It can be even tougher on the secretary who may feel caught in the middle.

For example, the reason one mother may consistently get into a deficit situation is because other mothers in the network do not feel comfortable with her parenting style or her home environment. If members fear their child will be placed with a mother they don't respect, they won't use the co-op at all.

One way to get around this is to allow women to arrange their own sits directly with other mothers. Then, all that's needed is for the sitter to notify the secretary once the sit has taken place. The secretary's only responsibility, then, will be to add the appropriate number of hours to the sitter and subtract them from the gadder. (All of this is done on an honor system, of course.)

The only time the secretary would arrange sits is if a member wants her to do it, either because she's been unable to find someone herself or because she doesn't want to take the time to do so. Each month, the secretary provides the members with a complete list of how many hours everyone has gadded and sat.

It may sound like the secretary is the poor overworked slave of the group, the most dreaded job in the world. Far from it! In most groups, everyone anxiously awaits their chance to be secretary. Why? Because it's relatively easy to do and you get credit for doing it! For every hour you spend serving the co-op, you can credit yourself one hour to be used for future babysitting needs.

A major advantage of the secretarial system is that it keeps everyone involved and keeps the network balanced. Cliques are a very real danger. They can destroy your co-op because new members will quickly drop out, sensing they are being left out. Long-term members, who realize they aren't part of the "in" crowd will eventually get fed up, too. The secretarial system is also a lifesaver for those dear, sweet moms who just can't say no. And it's a deterrent to members who would like to use the co-op without giving back.

Coupon System

Our co-op uses the coupon system for one simple reason: it's so simple. When a new member pays her $5.00 entry fee, she receives twenty coupons worth half an hour each. It is up to her to arrange sitting and gadding. There's no record keeping because members simply exchange coupons. If someone runs out, she may borrow from the central "hour card bank" (more on that later), although doing so is discouraged. Instead, members who are running low on coupons should place a "request for sitting" notice in the co-op newsletter or use whatever means is arranged to communicate a shortage of coupons.

The disadvantage is that mothers who really need the co-op, yet keep running out of coupons, may simply drop out. Also, no one has any sense of who is or is not using the co-op. A woman may feel she is being left out, when in fact, no one is using the co-op. And, of course, no one will reach out when they feel left out . . . instead, they'll drop out. In that case, the co-op is doomed to die a premature death—and no one even knows it. It will just fade away like so many other well-intentioned endeavors. And, in fact, this untimely death syndrome is the biggest disadvantage of the coupon system. If you decide to use this approach, make sure you have some way of assuring that members are, in fact, actively using the co-op. Otherwise, women will withdraw and become more isolated than they were in the first place.

One possible solution is card counts. Assign someone to call around periodically to determine how many cards each member has. She can then issue a report at the next meeting. Better yet, she can take the responsibility to match up those with too many cards and those who do not have enough cards.

Another problem for new members is breaking into the established circle. In other words, women will begin relying on just one or two other members and never seek to expand their relationships. Since they've got their babysitting arrangements all figured out, it's almost impossible for new members to find their place in the network. The result is a high turnover rate. Women who want to become active members eventually grow discouraged and drop out.

Mothers Only?

Some groups decide that only mothers can participate or serve as sitters. Others feel child-care providers, such as a nanny, are welcome to bring children to outings or sit with a child. Whichever you decide, you'll need to spell out the guidelines to the members upon joining the network.

Our network occasionally has a father or two at special events, and one dad even participates in our babysitting co-op. Another member's nanny has cared for my Leah just beautifully.

Yet, some groups insist mothers only is the way to go. If for some reason a mom can't make it, another mom may bring her child to the event. But the mother cannot send a substitute caregiver. The rationale is that the mothers want to form friendships. To do so, they must feel free to talk openly. If there are constantly new faces in the crowd, that's hard to do. Only your network can decide what's right for you.

Make It Official

Whichever option seems best to you, make it official. Informal co-ops can survive, but they have an uphill battle from day one. Instead, spell out the rules and regulations from the very beginning. Make sure all new members know exactly what they can expect from the network, and more importantly, what's expected from them.

Chapter 15 includes sample rules and regulations that you can use. Some of the rules may seem too strict or arbitrary, but I assure you they are the fruit of much thought and many years of accumulated experience. You should feel free to make adjustments; however, it would be a good idea to begin with the guidelines we offer. Then, as your network becomes more established, you can change any of the rules to suit your own needs by a majority vote of the membership.

You might also want to investigate the National MOMS Club, which is a nationwide, nonprofit support group designed specifically for at-home mothers. Call their headquarters to find out if there is a chapter near you. If not, you can start one for a very reasonable fee. The real advantage of linking your local network with the National **MOMS** Club is that they provide you with local, regional, and national coordinators who can help you get your chapter off the ground. These are experienced leaders who know the challenges you face when starting a new club. When questions and concerns arise, help is just a phone call away.

You can contact them at:

NATIONAL MOMS CLUB
814 Moffatt Circle
Simi Valley, CA 93065
(805) 526–2725

If you think connecting with a nationwide support network makes sense for you, be sure to contact them prior to your first organizational meeting. They have their own leader's manual and by-laws. Otherwise, you can use the material included in Chapter 15. During your first meeting, you should carefully review your group's rules and explain why they are important. Then, each time you add a new member, discuss the rules during her home visit.

Take Time for Reflection

1. Do you prefer the secretarial or coupon system?_____
(If you have gathered a core group of members, conduct a survey.)

2. List women you know who might eventually meet the requirements for each of these positions. Remember, if your network starts small (and many groups prefer to *stay* small), you will not need all of these formal positions. However, you can still assign these tasks on an informal basis.

POSITION	BEST WOMAN FOR THE JOB
President	_____
Vice-President	_____
Secretary	_____
Hospitality	_____
Membership	_____
Social Events	_____
Special Concerns	_____
Publicity	_____
Newsletter Editor	_____

12

Beware the "Attack of the Killer Mom"

"NOTHING CAN KILL a group faster—in spirit, if not in actuality—than the formation of cliques," insists Mary James, Founder of the National **MOMS** Club. Cliques are hard to define, but you know one when you see one. You especially know the feeling you get when you realize you're not part of the clique. Who wants to feel left out in the cold? No one, and that's why people will stop coming to your group.

Cliques: the Kiss of Death

You know you've got a clique on your hands when it's hard for new people to break in. It's a clique when visitors are ignored and shut out of the conversation. If you want your network to grow, you have to make new people feel welcomed and honored. You may think, we don't want our network to grow; we're happy just the way we are. Here's the bad news: any network that isn't growing is dying. It may not be immediately obvious, but it's only a matter of time before rigor mortis sets in.

To remedy clique-ishness, make sure everyone is encouraged to participate. There's a time for special friendships; and there's a time for *group interaction*. Understanding the difference is what sets grown women apart from high school girls. If your mothers' network has more than ten members, you should assign an official Hospitality Chairperson, who will make sure new people receive the special attention they deserve.

Assign a newsletter editor to keep everyone informed of events. One of her first jobs should be to write profiles of all existing members. Then as new members join, she can write them up in the newsletter. Not only will they feel honored, but the existing members will have solid information to connect with. You can also distribute copies of everyone's completed Personality Profiles (see Chapter 8). This will help women discover their common interests.

What if the Clique Has Already Formed?

If a clique has already formed, you need to take immediate action. It's hard when you're on the outside, but here are some strategies that might just work:

- Understand why the clique members are behaving that way. It is because *they* are insecure, so don't be intimidated by them.
- Realize they are not going to draw you into their circle. Instead, you'll have to draw them out.
- Refuse to be part of the clique, even if you are welcomed into it.
- Only talk to one person in the clique at a time; refuse to get into a group dynamic with them.
- Invite one of the women to lunch and get to know her. Try to draw her into a positive relationship with you.
- When you have get-togethers, only invite one member of the clique.
- If you are in a position of formal authority within the network, gently talk to them about how their behavior is affecting others. If you are not in a position of authority, encourage someone who is to take action. The problem will not get better on its own.

- One effective strategy is to ask the women for their suggestions on making new members feel welcome. For example, you might say, "It's obvious that you, Susan, Tammy, and Barbara have a very special relationship. I know a lot of other women in our group would like to enjoy that sense of belonging. Do you have any suggestions?" As they begin to brainstorm ideas, they may realize how they have failed to welcome other women in the past.

- Encourage them to reach out. For example, if you ask them for ideas on welcoming new women and they suggest follow-up phone calls or a one-on-one meeting, simply turn the tables. Ask: "Would you be willing to follow up like that?" As she takes an active role as part of the solution, she'll be less likely to continue being part of the problem.

Gossip

We've all heard it before; we've all done it before. "She said that you said that she said that you said. . . ." It's gossip and it's an insidious poison. Again, don't let the gossips intimidate you. Instead, understand that it is a sign of weakness. Jan Whaley, former Director of Women's Ministries at Bethany Community Church in Tempe, Arizona, says, "A woman who is gossiping or having a negative impact is crying for attention. Somewhere her feelings have been hurt, or she's been wounded in some way. Gossip is her way of getting even. Or it might be a way to draw attention and make herself feel important. The most insecure women in your network will cause the most trouble, because they are easily offended and likely to lash out. So rather than get angry with them, you need to reach out and encourage them."

"Sometimes people want to talk about relationships or situations just to get a reality check," observes Lynne Rienstra, a pastor's wife from Cape Cod. "And that's fine, as long as you don't name names or provide enough detail so that the other party can figure out who you mean. The minute you do that, you've crossed the boundary. Making judgments about another person is very dangerous territory. It's no job for mere mortals, because we can't possibly know all the facts.

"Often women will couch gossip in terms of concern for another woman," says Lynne. She advises, "Stop the person and ask, 'Have you talked to her directly about this?' There are very few situations where it's legitimate to talk about someone else behind her back. All that does is build barriers between people. We have to have the courage to say to the gossiper, 'I feel really uncomfortable hearing this.' Stop and consider, 'Would I want someone to be talking about me this way?' If the answer is no, don't do it."

Dispute Resolution

In some cases, a dispute may arise between two women who simply cannot resolve it between themselves. That's why it's so important to have a formal leadership structure. When there is a system in place for dealing with grievances, women feel more secure. They know they have a place to turn before the problem gets completely out of hand. And when women feel like they have an outlet, they'll be less likely to pour out their venom elsewhere.

Handling Conflicts Between Children

The best way to handle conflicts between children is to prevent them in the first place. Young children, especially, are not fond of sharing. So if your child has a special toy, and you're scheduled to sit, put the toy away. Likewise, do not send your child's favorite toy along. It seems like a great idea, because it will bring comfort. But you can bet the sitter's child will want that toy and then . . . look out. Better to say mommy *forgot* it, than for your child to see the other child *got* it.

Another possibility is to provide similar toys, especially for children aged two to three. That way, they can have their toy and share it, too. (Some might argue that this will breed selfishness, but it will also prevent bloodshed.) Of course, a parent should intervene immediately if a conflict does occur. Preschool children should not be left to slog it out on their own. They need a mother's help to resolve the situation in relative peace.

If you are consistently having problems with a child when you gad, it's best to tell the mother. (Any child can have a bad day, but if you notice a pattern of behavior, it's time to speak up.) Do not let your frustration and concern build up over time. And don't gossip behind her back. Nothing is worse for a mother than when her child is blacklisted and she doesn't know why. That does not mean ignore the situation. It means confront it firmly, but with a loving attitude.

This is not the time to attack the mother, place blame, or warn her that her child is bound for juvenile court. Instead, offer constructive suggestions that have worked for you in the past. Also, be sure you understand what type of discipline she expects you to use when her child misbehaves (i.e., time out, etc.).

Helen Sturm has been involved in various women's groups in churches and neighborhoods in Colorado. She says pretending the problem doesn't exist is not a real solution. Instead, you have to talk it out with the other mother. But be sure to go in a loving manner. It's not what you say, but how you say it that matters. You might say something like, 'I'm concerned about this situation, because your child is special and you're a special mom. Let's make this work.' "

Avoiding the issue would be much easier, of course. "That's when you make the choice," explains Helen. "Am I really committed to making this relationship work? Or do I just want to move on to the next friend? Think it through carefully. If you take that attitude, you will run through everyone in the neighborhood real quick! Because kids are kids and conflicts are part of it.

"It's so important for the mothers to talk to each other if their children are experiencing conflict. And they need to talk together with the children. However, this has to be done privately and with sensitivity. In our group, both moms would sit down with the children involved. We'd say something like, 'Mamas don't always do things just right either. Let's pray and ask God to help us to love each other more, and tell Him we are sorry for fighting.' "

Helen recalls, "We started doing this with our children when they were two or three years old. They understand so much more than we even realize. We'd pray with them, then everyone would hug and make up."

Renegade Toddler

Max McKee has established quite a reputation in the neighborhood—and he is only two years old. "We think he may be the Tasmanian Devil," confesses his mother, Dorrie. "Max has been in constant motion from the time I carried him." Recently, Dorrie dropped Max off with Anita, a fellow co-op member, so she could go to a doctor's appointment.

Dorrie returned to discover that Max had bitten Anita's three-year-old son, Ryan, in the face. "He actually drew blood!" she exclaims. "Anita wasn't even sure how it happened. She turned her back for one minute and the next thing she knew Ryan was bleeding." When Ryan tried to cover the wound on his cheek, Max proceeded to bite him on the hand.

"I felt so guilty," recalls Dorrie. "Isn't guilt a parent's middle name? Logically, I knew I couldn't have controlled the situation. I wasn't even there when it happened, but I felt totally responsible. I couldn't believe my child had caused such a major trauma to another kid in the neighborhood. I felt helpless. It's hard enough to control them when you are around, let alone when you're not."

Dorrie said the situation got worse when she ran home and gathered up some antibiotic cream and Band-Aids. "I took them over to Anita's house right away. I gave Ryan the cream and the adhesive bandages with Big Bird and Cookie Monster, thinking that would make him feel better. Well, he didn't like the bandages so Anita took them off. When she did, it ripped the wound and hurt like the dickens. So here I am trying to be nice, trying to fix the situation and my Band-Aid hurt the kid. I just couldn't get it right."

Dorrie was "incredibly embarrassed in front of Anita and the other mothers in the neighborhood." She was afraid the other women in the group would not want to associate with her or her son anymore. I thought, "Gee, is that what these women think I'm teaching my child. It was awkward at first, because the whole neighborhood was talking about the biting incident."

Fortunately, the other moms reached out to reassure Dorrie. "They made me feel so much better about it. A number of women called me and got me laughing about it. They let me know that it wasn't my fault; that it didn't mean I was a bad mother or a bad person. One friend, Jennifer, put things in perspective when she said, 'Hey look, some kids are hitters. Some kids are biters. Max is the biter, that's all.'

"The next time I dropped Max off with one of the moms, I warned her, 'He really is a very sweet child, but he's been known to bite.' "

Today, the biting incident is nothing more than a neighborhood joke. It *could* have been blown out of proportion and caused strife between the mothers. Dorrie and Anita are living proof that conflicts between children do not have to become conflicts between the mothers. Dorrie believes she and Anita were able to work things out—and encourage their sons to work things out—because they are both active in the playgroup. They have spent enough time watching the children in action, so they are realistic enough to recognize that no one's child is a perfect little angel. "We've learned to tolerate the antics of each other's children," explains Dorrie. As with all other aspects of motherhood, as you learn to resolve conflict between your children, you will learn more about yourself in the process.

Take Time for Reflection

1. Are you guilty of clique-ishness? Is it difficult for new moms to join? If so, indicate how you can begin to demonstrate a more welcoming attitude to women outside your circle of friends:

_____

_____

_____

_____

_____

_____

2. Have others in your network formed a clique? If so, review the suggestions for dealing with cliques included in this chapter. Note which strategies you might use to encourage the clique members to adopt a more welcoming attitude:

_____

_____

_____

_____

3. Have you been guilty of gossiping about someone? Is there anything you can do to repair whatever damage you may have caused? Take time to reflect upon this.

_____

_____

_____

_____

_____

_____

4. If you are in a position of leadership, what measures will you take to insure women in your network have a recourse for resolving conflicts?

_____

_____

_____

_____

_____

_____

5. Are there any children in your neighborhood in conflict with your child? Consider whether or not it is time to approach the child's mother and seek to resolve the situation.

_____

_____

_____

_____

_____

Part Four

The Wrap-Up

13
Special Projects

THROUGHOUT *No More Lone Ranger Moms*, we have touched upon the importance of doing special projects with other women. On the following pages, I will give you specific examples of activities you can do with two or more other women. The range of special projects you can enjoy is limited only by your imagination. See which activities you might enjoy doing with other women in your church or community.

Cook-a-thons and Shared Meals

Most mothers would agree that the hour before mealtime is the worst time of day. If you are like me, chances are you spend the day in denial. "This is the day six o'clock won't come. If I don't think about it, dinnertime will pass and no one will notice." Yet, strangely enough, it rolls around every single day and I have to do something about it.

Before I heard about the book *Once-a-Month Cooking* by Mimi Wilson and Mary Beth Lagerborg (Focus on the Family, 1992), I lived in constant dread of the words, "Honey, what's for dinner?" (After fourteen years of my cooking, you would think my husband would know better than to ask with such hopefulness in his voice.) I'm still not a big fan of cooking, but I have found an easier way. I set aside one or two Saturdays per month and get the vast majority of my cooking done. Sound impossible? Well, not only is it possible, you can even make it fun. Well, not exactly fun, but. . . .

Mary Beth reports that women all over the country are gathering in church kitchens to prepare a month's worth of meals. "It's a lot more fun if you get together and divide up the work. Play some uplifting music, roll up your shirtsleeves, and make a day of it," she suggests. Mary Beth also advises recruiting someone to watch the children. "Whether you leave them at one woman's house or at home with Dad, you'll get a lot more done in less time if you can concentrate on the business at hand."

Another option, of course, is to bring an older child (or several older children, as needed) to babysit the younger ones. Simply arrange to take over the church nursery along with the church kitchen. All the moms can chip in to pay the sitters and it will be money very well spent. After all, by buying in bulk and cooking one month's worth of meals in advance, you will be saving a significant amount of money on your grocery bill.

Before gathering in the church (or community center) kitchen, you will need to organize your materials and develop a clear strategy for the day. First, assign each woman a portion of the shopping list. For example, one person will buy all the produce, another will buy meat, and another will buy canned goods, etc. You will also want to bring along an ample number of freezer bags and other storage containers. You may want to invest the additional money required to purchase disposable containers to make dividing the food much simpler. You should each save your receipts, total the bill, and divide by the number of women participating.

Mary Beth reports that "some women's groups prepare a one-month menu and put all of the food in the church freezer. They use disposable containers and include cooking instructions with each dish. That way, when a need arises in the church, meals are ready." I guess I'm just not that noble, because if I cook all day, I'll want to take some food home with me. Your network might want to do a combination, as Becky Albrecht of Exton, Pennsylvania, does.

As the mother of seven children, Becky knows what it's like to spend time in the kitchen . . . and plenty of it. Her friends Paula (six children) and Susie (seven children) were in the same boat. So they decided to make the task more enjoyable by doing it together. "Among the three of us, we have twenty-six people to cook for. So we get together every week to prepare bulk meals," says Becky. "We take turns cooking at each others' houses, and we bring all the kids along. It's a good opportunity for them to play together because we all home school."

The women follow a very informal system, but often Susie buys most of the food. However, all of the mothers stay alert to bargains at the supermarket. If they catch a good sale item, they will stock up for everyone. Sometimes they divide the cost, but not always. "Our friendship is close enough that we don't feel a need to keep score. Our goal is to support one another and that's understood. The rest seems to fall into place on its own," says Becky.

"One time, Susie bought all the meatballs and sauce and we made huge pots of spaghetti. Another time, I found chicken on sale and bought what we would need to make breaded chicken." Unlike the plans developed by Mary Beth Lagerborg, Becky and her friends say they only tackle one type of food at a time. As a result, they can finish their cooking within a few hours. "When you're cooking for twenty-six people, it's simpler that way," notes Becky.

"We gather in the kitchen to talk and have a wonderful time," she says. "And the kids have a blast. But at the same time, we get the work done. When we're finished, we have one dinner for each of our families, and two meals to share with someone in need. At that point, we ask: 'Who do we know who needs a meal?' Someone who recently had a baby or perhaps a medical problem. There's always someone in need. So, whoever lives nearest to the person will drop off the extra meals. We're helping each other, but we're also reaching out to serve others."

Why not get together with a couple of friends and make one or two of your favorite recipes? It's a fun way to beat the Lone Ranger Mom syndrome.

Clothing Exchange

What should you do with clothes you no longer wear but which are still in good condition? Why not exchange them with other women? That's exactly what the women of Bethany Community Church have been doing annually for the last few years. Beth Werner, current Chairman of Women's Ministry, offers these suggestions. "Tell the women to bring only clean, slightly used clothing. We allow two weeks for everyone to drop off their items at the church. Then we recruit thirty women to help organize the clothes on a Friday night, in preparation for the Saturday event."

Finding volunteers is much easier than Beth had initially expected. "We tell them they get first pick of the clothes the night before. We have no trouble attracting volunteers. The clothes are sorted by men's, women's, and children's sizes." At the last event the women filled the entire gymnasium with seven large clothing racks, fifteen large tables, plus bleachers overflowing with clothes.

On Saturday morning they threw open the doors to the church gymnasium and let anyone who wanted to come take whatever they wanted. "There were absolutely no rules," says Beth. "We called it The Great Clothing Giveaway. It was neat to see how much fun our own women had. But it was even more meaningful to help people who clearly were in desperate need of clothes. One woman came in and tried on a dress I had donated. When she left she was just beaming with pride. Several people came in to gather clothes for Crisis Pregnancy Centers and homeless shelters."

Beth says even though they only promoted the event through their own church, the word spread quickly. On the day of the event, the women put a large poster with balloons on the local highway, pointing toward the church. "A lot of people drove in off the street," says Beth. "One gentleman picked out three suits, three shirts, and three ties; they were all in excellent condition. As he turned to leave, he confessed, 'I feel like I'm stealing.' But he obviously needed career clothes, and he sure found them."

Another highlight of the day was when three air-conditioning repairmen, who were working at the church, stopped by. One worker's wife had just had a baby, and they were picking out baby clothes. Beth recalls, "It was a kick to watch these three big men stooping over the infant table, picking out little booties.

"At the end of the day, a man came in from a church in South Phoenix (a poor, inner city neighborhood). He asked if he could take what was left, we loaded up his van and off he went. It was really an exciting end to the event, knowing we were able to minister to another church with far fewer resources."

You may not be able to plan a clothing exchange as elaborate as Bethany Community—which has several thousand members. Nevertheless, you can certainly set up a small exchange in one woman's house. You will have a lot of fun and save money in the process.

Health Food Co-op

Did you know that modern-day co-ops date back to October 24, 1844, when twenty-eight members of the Rochdale Equitable Pioneers Society formed a co-op in England? Today, in the United States, over 100 million people are members of food cooperatives. Worldwide, there are now 700 million members of cooperatives. Why? Because it just makes sense.

By joining forces with other families you can buy good food in large quantities, thus enjoying a price break. You also enjoy the companionship of other women who share your concern for good eating. "It is a way for people to get to know one another. In the spirit of old-time barn raising and quilting bees it is a way for people to work together to satisfy the needs of many. It also provides an opportunity to learn the skills necessary for working effectively and fairly with other people" (*Stocking Up*, Winter Issue 1994, p. 10).

That's what Judy Blankenbeckler discovered when she organized a food co-op in 1980 at New Life Presbyterian Church in Jenkintown, Pennsylvania. "It started in my house," she recalls. "I wanted to provide my family with healthy food, but I was frustrated because the prices at the health food stores were so much higher than the local grocery. At that time, health food stores were few and far between."

Judy and a friend researched where various health foods were produced, and they went directly to the factories and distributors to buy in large quantities. Then they broke the food down into smaller quantities and divided it between their two families. The co-op quickly grew to a dozen families.

"One month, we organized and sent out everyone's orders. The next month, it would come in and be divided. We required everyone to pay when they placed their order. We sold the leftovers to any member who wanted to buy. We didn't sell anything at a profit. But everyone had to volunteer a certain amount of time based on how much they ordered. For example, a $30 order required one hour of work; $60 required two hours, etc. A coordinator handled the work schedule to make sure people followed up on their commitments. Another person reviewed the order sheets to determine what was needed, check the money, etc. Another person supervised the breakdown of the food into bags and packages. Yet another coordinated the cleanup after the session. Although it didn't start out that way, it eventually became a highly organized system.

"Two days a month, everyone came to our house and divided the food into bags. We had rice, beans, flour, nuts, tea, spices, honey, powdered milk, and other healthy non-perishables. Co-op members donated bags for packaging everything. When the co-op grew past thirty families, we began working out of our church," recalls Judy.

The New Life Food Co-op charged a $5 membership fee to each family. That helped cover administrative costs. Work schedules were strictly enforced. "If people didn't pull their weight, they had to do double work next time. If they still didn't meet their obligations, they were out. We'd simply say, 'We're sorry about that, but we show no mercy around here!' "

At its peak, the co-op had 60 families involved and ordered around $4,000 worth of food each time. "It saved everyone a lot of money and we all enjoyed healthy meals," explains Judy. "It was also fun (well, hard fun) to get together and dig into flour up to our elbows. We were also able to buy first-quality food, fresh from the factory. That's something most of us would not have been able to afford."

A number of women in my network use the Tucson Cooperative Warehouse (TCW) of Tucson, Arizona, to purchase health foods in bulk. TCW now serves Arizona, New Mexico, and parts of Texas, Colorado, Utah, Nevada, and California. To find similar health food suppliers in your area, check the Yellow Pages.

The Tucson Cooperative Warehouse offers the following suggestions for organizing a health food co-op (from *Stocking Up*, Winter 1994, pp. 10–11):

A typical buying club operates like this:

1. Members make up their household orders.
2. Those household orders are combined to meet the wholesale minimum on each item.
3. The group order is phoned or mailed to the warehouse or supplier. Members may prepay at this time. (NOTE: Some groups travel to a nearby co-op facility and make their purchases directly.)
4. The paperwork used at the food distribution is prepared, if it hasn't already been done.
5. Your group picks up its order at the warehouse or meets the delivery truck locally and pays for the order with a single, group check.
6. Members meet to divide the order into individual household orders. Bulk foods are divided or cut, weighed, and packaged, and are distributed with prepackaged goods to members.
7. Household invoices are adjusted: prices are corrected, cheese or produce prices are added, any out-of-stock items are deleted, extras are added, and the invoice is totaled.
8. When distribution is done, the site and equipment are cleaned.
9. Members pay for their orders, if they haven't already, and take their food home.
10. Any final internal bookkeeping is completed.
11. The coordinator contacts the warehouse if any problems or complaints arise.

Sharing the work fairly is the key to a successful food

co-op. Working together for everyone's benefit is what co-ops are all about. The group benefits from the talents and skills of many and is healthier when not dependent on a few.

Each member can contribute by doing at least one job. Working actually increases a member's commitment to their co-op. They enjoy the satisfaction of doing their fair share and the camaraderie of working together. Clearly defining the jobs and the time involved makes it easier for busy members to commit to their buying club responsibilities.

If members in your group place written orders, indicate a minimum and maximum number for each item. The minimum indicates the fewest you want to get. The maximum indicates the most you would be willing to get and pay for. The bigger the spread between these two amounts, the more flexibility the order compilers have and the greater chance the co-op will actually reach the minimum wholesale amount and be able to order that item. This system of ordering is referred to as the minimum/maximum or min/max system. Use it to help everyone get what they want from your food co-op.

Home School Co-op

The most amazing thing happens at Dawn Brown's home every other Tuesday: it is transformed into a schoolroom from 8:30 A.M. to 3:00 P.M. Twelve children, ranging in age from third grade to high school freshmen, gather to learn from one of five participating mothers. "We start the day with an hour of dance. We hire people to teach clogging, country western, and tap dancing. And, yes, the moms dance along. One of the mothers teaches Spanish for an hour to all children and the moms."

Dawn says she has never studied so hard in her life. In May, two of the families are going on a one-week mission trip to southern Mexico to minister among the mountain Indians. One of the women has a sister who is a missionary there.

In preparation, the families have spent the last year collecting clothing to give to the orphans. They have also learned songs in Spanish.

Currently, the children are studying geography with one of the fathers as instructor. They have a one-hour geography lesson, followed by a lunch break. In the afternoon, they do hands-on geography projects. Dawn explains, "This year we're studying countries of the world by continent. At the end of two years, the children will be able draw the entire world in complete detail— that includes countries, mountains, rivers, and other geographic features."

Each of the mothers has taken full responsibility for teaching one of the continents. They find all the materials, including books, articles, puzzles, and lesson plans. They also develop appropriate crafts the children can make. Sharing the teaching responsibility makes everyone's job easier.

"In the beginning I home schooled alone," says Dawn. "But the kids needed the socialization. The moms also benefit because we get together twice a week to encourage one another. If I were doing this myself, I'd have to come up with something every week out of the year. Now, I only have to worry about six or eight weeks' worth of lesson plans."

One of Dawn's partners, Kim, agrees: "It's hard to make the extra effort when it's just your own children. It motivates you to know you are responsible to all the other moms and all the children. We have a wealth of resources within the seven families that we just would not have on our own."

I home school our daughter, Leah, so I know how lonely it can get sometimes. The great thing about forming a home school co-op is that it guards against the most common pitfalls and/or charges made against home schooling:

1. Opportunities for Socialization. As soon as you say you are home schooling your child(ren), everyone wants to talk about social skills. I firmly believe children can best learn proper social conduct from their parents, not a room filled with 30 of their peers. Nevertheless, children do crave social interaction with their peers. A home school co-op is the perfect way to provide interaction, while still exercising parental control over the environment.

2. Time and Energy Saving. People often argue that they could not possibly find time to plan enough home school lessons for a full school year. Well, divide and conquer like Dawn Brown and company! By joining forces with other mothers (fathers, too), you can reduce the amount of preparation time required from each parent.

3. Cost Saving. Ever wonder why so many home schooling mothers also operate a home business? Home schooling can be E-X-P-E-N-S-I-V-E. All the curricula and supplies quickly start to add up. This is a great time to be educating your children at home, because there are so many resources and tools available. Unfortunately, gazing through all those full-color catalogs can become a high-priced and highly addictive hobby! (Believe me, I know!)

So how do you access all the latest and greatest home school furnishings without going bankrupt? Your home school co-op, of course! By joining forces and finances with other home schooling moms, you can turn all those must-have items into reality. Even if you don't teach cooperatively, you can share curriculum and other tools with your network of home school moms. I am constantly exchanging books, magazines, and curriculum with other moms—it just makes good sense.

If you do decide to form a home school co-op, you can hardly ask for a better how-to guide than *No More Lone Ranger Moms*. Virtually every idea contained herein can be tailored to the needs of home schooling moms.

4. Access to Experts. Anyone with enough desire can teach the basics to little ones . . . but what about high school science? What about music? No parent in the world has expertise in every area. Once again, your home school co-op comes to the rescue. When five families join together, you have access to ten parents, twenty grandparents, dozens of aunts and uncles, countless friends, neighbors, and colleagues. Suddenly you have an incredible network of contacts and resources to draw upon.

5. Motivation for Students. Keeping your home schooled student motivated can be tough for some parents because their children don't seem to have any interest in learning. Life becomes a constant battle to keep their home school afloat. Some parents even resort to bribes or find themselves forever meting out discipline. Thus far, Leah has been extremely self-motivated, but the day may come when her enthusiasm wanes. That's just the time I will start truly *needing* a home school co-op.

In the context of a co-op, other parents and fellow students can keep each other motivated. Fresh ideas and a fresh perspective often work miracles.

6. Motivation for Moms. Time for true confessions: sometimes *Mom* needs some extra motivation. There have been many days at the Partow ranch when I've had to drag myself through the day's lesson. Other times I have covered the bare minimum, when a little extra planning and effort could have made the lesson extra special. Again, a home school co-op can save the day. Knowing that the other mothers and their children are counting on you can be a real motivator. And the enthusiasm of the other moms can be just the tonic needed for your sagging spirits.

If you have ever thought about home schooling, or if you have been trying to make it on your own, why not join forces with other mothers in your church or community? Even if you don't want to teach cooperatively, you can still build a home schooling mothers' support network using the information provided in this book. Remember: You don't have to be a Lone Ranger mom just because you're a home schooling mom.

Find Your Own Special Project

What types of special projects appeal to you? Perhaps a clothing exchange? How about starting a health food co-op or organizing a cook-a-thon? The ideas included above are just that: ideas. You and the women in your support network can use them as a springboard for developing projects that meet your unique needs. Whatever you do, the important thing is working together for the common good. No more of that Lone Ranger stuff!

14
Moms Helping Moms

SINCE THE RELEASE of my first book, *Home-made Business*, I have been invited to participate in dozens of small business conferences around the country. I began to notice that all the conferences had one thing in common: a session on networking. That's because independent business owners quickly discover that although their goal is to *make it on their own, they can't make it all alone.* In order to succeed without relying on a corporation to provide a steady paycheck, millions of Americans have learned to create their own support systems.

Some Thoughts on Networking

Once I realized the importance of networking, I began searching for the most effective techniques. In the process, I developed Five Golden Rules for Networking Success. They served me well as a home-based businesswoman, and I was able to surround myself with a group of people who became my business lifeline. I call them my strategic partners. They are committed to helping me succeed, and I am equally committed to their success. When a business deal goes sour, I know who to call for a pep talk. When I need to prepare for an important speech, I know where to go for a free coaching session. In short, whatever needs arise in my business, I know exactly where to turn.

Yet, as a mother, I often found myself floundering— unsure where to turn when I needed help. Then, one day when I was preparing to deliver a presentation on business networking, a light bulb went on. *Couldn't I apply these same principles to my mothers' support network? After all, my work as a mother is far more difficult and far more important than any business deal. Wouldn't it be great if I could find strategic partners to support me as a mother?* The answer, I believe, is a resounding yes. That's why I want to share with you the Five Golden Rules for Networking Success . . . as applied to the business of motherhood.

1. Do Unto Others. Here's a universal principle that works whenever and wherever it is applied. If you want other moms to help you, then you must first be willing to help them. If you want someone to bring you a casserole when you bring your new baby home, then make sure you bring casseroles to other new moms.

2. Ask and You Shall Receive. So often, our needs go unmet because people don't know the circumstances we are facing. We expect other people to read our minds or to stay in touch with our daily crises, but that is unrealistic. If you need help, ask for it—and be very specific. Most women are eager to lend a helping hand, *when they are told exactly how to help.* Do you need a babysitter? Do you need a friend to talk to? Do you need some groceries but the car broke down? Is your toddler driving you crazy and you are afraid of losing your cool *big time?* Be humble enough to ask for help, and you'll be pleasantly surprised by the response.

3. Do Good Work. If you make a casserole . . . make your *best* casserole, and bring along salad and dessert for good measure. If a friend calls for a pep talk, give her encouragement, then follow up with a thoughtful card or gift. If you babysit, do something extra special with the children. Make a craft, paint rocks, color a beautiful card for mommy—go the extra mile.

4. Give Thanks. An attitude of gratitude will go a long way toward strengthening your strategic partnerships. We all want to feel appreciated and valued, and there's no such thing as being too grateful. When another mom goes out of her way to help you, go out of your way to show her your appreciation. A thank you note or a pretty postcard takes only a couple of minutes and a few cents—but it can mean so much.

5. Practice Patience. Now here's the hard part! You may be all excited about the power of moms helping moms. And you probably want to jump right in and start building your network. That's terrific! Just remember, friendship takes time, and most Americans are not used to forming the type of sacrificial relationship described in *No More Lone Ranger Moms*.

Also, remember that commitment is a dirty word to many people today. So don't expect everyone you meet to share your enthusiasm for mothers' support networks. Look patiently for the right women to support you on your journey. I've adopted the slogan from a shampoo commercial as my personal motto: "It won't happen overnight, but it will happen." My initial attempts at building a network were far from a smashing success. It took patience, understanding, and plenty of forgiveness.

Today, I can say without reservation that I am a better mother because of the women in my network. It has been worth all the time and tears I invested and I know it will be worth it for you, too. Moms helping moms can become a reality in your life, if only you will follow these Five Golden Rules.

15
Guidelines, Forms, and Resources

BABYSITTING CO-OP
RULES AND REGULATIONS

The following rules are adapted from the by-laws of the Red Mountain Ranch Mothers' Co-op located in Mesa, Arizona.

I. GENERAL

A. The co-op shall be limited to 60 members.
B. Prospective new members must:
1. Contact Board Member to receive application materials, Rules and Regulations, etc.
2. Agree to a Home Visit (see Board Member and review Safety Guidelines).

II. ORGANIZATION

There will be an annual election for all offices. Members must have been in the co-op for six months before serving as an officer. Nominations will be taken and then elected by a majority vote at the co-op's August meeting.

Any member not present at the meeting may not be nominated. A member has the right to refuse nomination. All officer terms shall run from September to September. Officers cannot run for two concurrent terms, but are not otherwise prohibited from holding future office. The President shall receive one half-hour card from each member at the end of her term.

If the network is new, the founder will serve as President for the first year. She will have the right to appoint all other officers, chairpersons, and coordinators, each for an annual term, on an as-needed basis. In subsequent years, all positions shall be elected. (NOTE: Initially, when the network is small, the President will handle many of the responsibilities assigned here to chairpersons and coordinators. As the network grows, the President should quickly delegate responsibilities to include as many members as possible in the operation of the co-op.)

A. President

1. Provide direction and leadership to officers and members.

2. Process prospective co-op members and follow procedures to assure they are aware of Rules and Regulations.

3. The President, along with the Vice-President, shall conduct a Home Visit for prospective members (see Section IV-Safety). The officers shall not bring their children to the Home Visit, but shall receive credit in hours for their time spent. It is the officer's responsibility to obtain the appropriate hour cards from the Hour Bank.

4. At Home Visits, officers shall tour the home and yard, and ask pertinent questions regarding safety precautions. A Home Visit Report shall be filed in the Co-op Book.

5. The President shall conduct all monthly meetings during her term. She should adhere to Roberts' Rules of Order to insure that all items are

voted on by the members.

6. The President shall enforce the Rules and Regulations and handle any infractions thereof.

7. Keep all co-op records current and Co-op Book complete (including newsletters, rosters, master sheets, emergency authorizations, new member packets, etc.).

8. Keep documentation of any special meetings that are called.

9. Update the master copy of the Rules and Regulations before the end of her term, as necessary.

10. Keep a list of members who have been notified of any infraction (in usage or otherwise), documentation of dates, follow-up calls needed, and any other pertinent information.

B. Vice-President

1. Assist President with Home Visits, monthly meetings, and any other necessary tasks.

2. Keep the Hour Card Bank and debit record.

3. Conduct a card count by phone prior to each quarterly meeting. Provide members and Newsletter Editor with an update.

4. Verify that all members have sit or gad at least twice per month, as per usage requirement described under Rule III, C–2.

5. Take minutes of the proceedings at monthly meetings. Maintain a record of minutes in the Co-op Book.

6. Seek to link members who have an excess of cards with those who have a shortage.

7. Maintain the Co-op Photo Album and bring it to the monthly meetings.

8. Coordinate special projects as needed.

9. Serve as officers' liaison to other chairpeople and coordinators.

C. Treasurer

1. Handle all monies collected or disbursed.

2. Count and verify monies upon transfer to suceeding Treasurer.

3. Responsible for the disposition of all monies while in her possession.

D. Membership Coordinator

1. Distribute information packets to prospective new members.

2. Notify the President to arrange a Home Visit.

3. Distribute Member Profile sheet to all new members. Ensure that they are promptly completed and given to the President to be placed in the Co-op Book.

4. Furnish Newsletter Editor with a copy of the completed profile, so editor can write a short article introducing the new member.

5. Update the master membership roster, and keep Newsletter Editor informed of any changes or deletions for the newsletter.

6. Furnish new member names to chairperson of activities in which the new members are interested.

7. Keep a "waiting list" of prospective members in the Co-op Book, and notify those waiting availability of park and pool days.

E. Hospitality Chairperson

1. Contact all new members by phone and inform them of co-op activities, encouraging them to participate.

2. Arrange transportation for new members to upcoming events, if needed.

3. Send greeting cards for appropriate occasions.

4. Furnish name tags with special markings to identify new members.

5. Arrange for all new members to be invited to lunch by an established co-op member who will become a mentor to the new member. The mentor will be responsible for helping the newcomer find her place within the co-op and insure that she feels welcome.

6. Oversee all mentors to make sure new members are receiving a proper welcome to the co-op.
7. Follow up with all members who miss the Quarterly Meeting.
8. Follow up with any member who appears to be inactive. Seek to integrate her back into the co-op.

F. Social Events Chairperson

1. Plan social activities for children, mothers, and couples, including Park Days, Moms' Night Out, Dinners for Eight, etc.
2. Plan an annual luncheon in honor of outgoing officers.
3. Arrange refreshments for the Quarterly Meeting.
4. Plan baby showers for expectant mothers.
5. Recruit other members, as needed, to assist with planning, hostessing, etc.
6. Actively encourage full participation in social events through phone calls, notices, etc.
7. Solicit suggestions from co-op members.

G. Special Concerns Chairperson

1. Schedule at least two full weeks of meals for all new mothers.
2. Schedule meals as needed for women who are ill or facing other challenging circumstances.
3. Arrange childcare (as needed) for children of new mothers or mothers who are ill.
4. Remain alert to special needs through contact with Hospitality Chairperson, mentors, and other means, as needed.
5. Handle phone calls from mothers with special needs. Then communicate these needs to other members via phone chain or as appropriate.

H. Publicity Chairperson

1. Identify publicity sources, including newspapers, radio, etc.
2. Prepare and submit monthly notices to local news media on upcoming events and general co-op information.

3. Arrange for black-and-white photos to be taken at all major events. Forward copies, along with a notice, to appropriate news media.
4. Maintain positive relations with local newspaper editor to insure positive coverage of the co-op's activities.
5. Update, edit, and distribute flyers promoting the co-op and its activities.

I. Newsletter Editor

The Newsletter Editor shall be appointed by the officers on an as-needed basis.

1. Compile and edit a monthly newsletter and calendar of events.
2. Newsletter should include a short article profiling each new member.
3. Distribute the newsletter to all members, by mail or personal delivery.
4. Editor will be reimbursed for expenses, but only as preapproved by the officers.

III. MEMBERSHIP REGULATIONS

A. Dues

1. Dues will be collected to cover the costs of operating the co-op. No officer or other member shall receive a salary or other form of payment. The only exception is reimbursement for expenses preapproved by the President or Treasurer.
2. Dues are $20.00 per year.
3. Dues must be paid upon joining (regardless of month) and renewed annually on the anniversary of membership. A check may be made payable to the President or to the co-op, if an account has been established. Dues must be paid current to remain in the co-op.

B. Meetings

1. All members are expected to attend monthly co-op meetings. Whenever possible, meetings will be

held during the day and babysitting will be provided. If it is impossible to attend, notification must be given to an officer prior to the meeting. Legitimate excuses will be accepted.

2. Failure to attend three *consecutive* meetings (even when notification has been given) will result in member being asked to resign.
3. Members should bring calendar, hour cards, paper, and pencil to monthly meetings.
4. The outgoing President will receive one half-hour card from each member.
5. Each member will donate one half-hour card to the co-op Hour Bank at the May and November monthly meetings. These half-hour cards will be used for periodic raffles and for payment to officers for Home Visits.
6. One member will be asked to volunteer her home for the next meeting, or an outside facility (church, clubhouse, other) may be used. Others will be asked to provide snacks and refreshments.
7. A special meeting may be called by the officers if it is deemed necessary to settle any disputes or issues before a regular meeting.
8. Meetings are open only to current co-op members.

C. Usage
   1. Each member must sit or gad (use a sitter) at least two times each month.
   2. Failure to sit or gad two times in a month constitutes inactive status. The first month a member is inactive, an officer will call, asking for activation of membership. A second lapse of usage will result in a request to activate membership within the following month. A third lapse of usage will result in the officers asking for member resignation.
   3. This rule excludes leaves of absence for vacations, illnesses, etc., and does not apply to the summer

months of June, July, or August.

D. Hours

1. Hour cards are used to pay the sitter for time spent sitting.

2. Each card has a value of one half hour.

3. Time is to be counted in half-hour increments. Hours are to be rounded off to the nearest half hour. Half-time will be paid for each additional child from one family. (Example: Mother with two children pays one and a half hours for each hour of babysitting. Mothers of three children pay two hours for each hour.) Time-and-a-half will be paid to sitter if the sit takes place at the gadder's residence.

4. A minimum of one hour constitutes a sit.

5. No Shows—Gadder will give sitter half the time originally arranged.

6. New members will be given twenty half-hour cards to start. (For a total of ten hours worth of co-op time.)

7. No provision will be made for lost hour cards. They are the sole responsibility of each member.

8. Five hours will be raffled off at each quarterly meeting. A member cannot win at two consecutive meetings and must be present to win.

9. Each member will bring one half-hour card to the May and November monthly meetings to donate to the Hour Bank.

10. Each member will also bring one half-hour card to each quarterly meeting to give to the outgoing President.

11. When a gadder goes into a debit situation while someone is sitting for her, the gadder must call the Vice-President to arrange for sitter payment from the Hour Bank for the portion of the sit that she shortchanged the sitter. The gadder's debit to the co-op Bank will be recorded in the

Co-op Book, and must be repaid before gadding again.

12. If a member has a negative balance of hours, she may ask the Newsletter Editor to include a request for sitting in the next newsletter.

13. The co-op Hour Bank and record book are maintained by the Vice-President. The Bank is used for distributing hour cards: to new members, to members needing a loan of hours, to officers for Home Visits, and to members winning the quarterly five-hour raffle.

14. If a member wishes to resign from the co-op, it is requested that she leave with ten hours (given to her at the start). Any hours that she is below ten should be paid to the co-op at $1.00 for each hour that she is in debt. Payment for hours is to be arranged with the officers. All hour cards must be returned to the officers.

E. Leaves of Absence and Resignations

1. Members may take a leave of absence by notifying the officers. An estimate of leave duration must be given. If the co-op is full, there is a three-month limit to leaves.

2. Members on leave must pay dues during the time on leave. They must also pay hours to the co-op Bank.

3. Resignation—the person leaving must turn in all remaining half-hour cards to the President. They will be required to pay $1.00 per hour for every hour less than ten (the total number of hours initially issued).

F. Grievance Procedure

1. Members will discuss any disputes or alleged irresponsibility at the time of occurrence between both parties involved. The problem will then be related to the officers as soon as possible. The officers will then take the following actions:

a. Determine whether the dispute is an infrac-

tion of co-op rules, or whether there was possible neglect on the part of the sitter, or if any
action was involved that might have endan-
gered the safety of any child.

    b. Temporarily suspend member until a special
meeting of all co-op members can be held to
vote on whether the action warrants termi-
nation from the co-op.

G. Associate Membership

Associate Membership shall be available to moms
who can't or don't want to sit, as well as to former members and new neighbors. Their children can attend parties for a small fee (to be decided by planning committee, dependent on costs involved for each event). These
members can receive the co-op newsletter for notice of
events for $5.00 per year to cover printing and distri-
bution costs. These members must do their own RSVP,
they will not be called before events. This includes children's events they want to participate in.

IV. SAFETY

A. Mandatory Safety Rules

    1. Each member must agree that in any emergency,
the sitter may call the child's personal physician
if they are unable to reach gadder or spouse. Permission for medical attention should be filled out
on the "Emergency Authorization Card" and
TAKEN WITH THE CHILD(REN) ON EVERY
SIT.

    2. Sitter must have liability insurance to cover med-
ical expenses for gadder's child in case of accident
or injury while at sitter's home.

    3. Backyards must be completely enclosed and all
fencing at least four feet high, and any gate or
door leading out of the yard must have a working
latch such that the gate or door cannot be opened
with a simple push.

4. Any permanent pool, spa, or fountain in the back-yard must meet the following safety standards:
   a. Must be separated from the yard on all sides by a four foot high fence. (Spa can have a childproof cover.)
   b. Any gate in the fence must be closed and LOCKED (not just latched, but LOCKED) at all times.
   c. There shall be no direct access from the house or garage to the pool area. If there are doors leading to the pool area, those members are required to make other members aware of the situation, and must have a secure lock on that door or window when sitting.
   d. If a pool, spa, or fountain is being constructed, the sitter is to let the gadder know this. Upon completion, the member is to notify the officers to change the roster information.
   e. Any temporary pool (above-ground pool, wading pool, spa, etc.) should either meet the same requirements as listed above for a permanent pool, or it must be drained at the time of the sit. A member with a non-complying temporary pool that cannot be drained must ask for a leave of absence during the time it is filled.

IMPORTANT NOTE: If there are members whose pools or other water hazards do not comply with the above rules, it is their responsibility to inform all gadders of this fact.

5. It is strongly suggested that no firearms be in the home of a co-op member. However, if there are any present, the following rules apply:
   a. Handguns must be kept in a locked box or container, and the key must be in a separate and secure location.
   b. Rifles must be kept in a locked gun rack or inaccessible location (like upper shelf of closet), with safety engaged.

    c. All ammunition must be kept locked and separate from firearms, with the key in a separate and secure location.

    d. BB guns are considered firearms, and the same rules apply.

    e. Members with firearms in their home MUST make all gadders aware of their presence.

6. It is strongly suggested that all medicines, cleaning products, alcohol-based cosmetics, or other poisonous substances shall be stored at least four and a half feet off the floor, or behind a childproof, locked cabinet door. If the member wishes to receive Toddler-Proof designation, this is required.

7. In areas in which access to harmful substances is made easier by permanent fixtures (i.e., climb on toilet to sink, to medicine cabinet) sitters are reminded to be extra attentive.

8. The garage is not required to be in compliance with #7 above. If it is not, however, the door to the garage must remain locked during a sit.

9. The sitter must inform the gadder if there are any stairs not blocked by an approved child safety gate.

10. There shall be at least one working smoke detector mounted on the wall or ceiling of the home.

11. Children must be attended at all times.

12. All children shall be watched only in the house or fenced backyard unless prior permission is obtained from the gadder. This means no walks, no playing in driveways, cul de sacs, etc., unless prior arrangements have been made.

13. Alcohol or drugs are absolutely forbidden to be used while sitting.

14. It is strongly advised not to take the gadder's child(ren) in your automobile because of the extra risk involved. If transportation is necessary during the sit, you must get prior approval from

the gadder; and state laws regarding the use of child safety seats and seat belts must be adhered to.

15. If a member wishes Toddler-Proof designation on the roster, her home must comply with a stricter set of guidelines than one who does not wish this designation. The Home Visit Report form details these guidelines.

NOTE: THE CO-OP DOES NOT HOLD RESPONSIBIL-ITY AS A GROUP FOR ACCIDENTS OR INJURIES.

V. PROCEDURES

1. When you need a sitter, contact a member and tell her the date and time you will be away.
2. It is important that the health of your child(ren) and family members be discussed between the sitter and gadder. A sick child from either household will require prior approval from both sitter and gadder.
3. IT IS THE PRIVILEGE OF ANY MEMBER TO REFUSE A SIT WITHOUT GIVING A REASON.
4. No one may sit for two or more families unless prior approval has been given by all parities involved. This includes all children, co-op members or not.
5. The gadder should give sitter information about her child(ren) such as allergies, fears of animals, potty training, special possessions, etc.
6. Before leaving to gad, it is IMPERATIVE that the sitter has your:
   a. Emergency Authorization Form
   b. Phone number where you can be reached. (If none is available, leave the phone number of a close friend or relative.)
7. Please remember to offer liquids to small children who cannot ask for them.
8. If you are not able to return at the time agreed

upon, you must call and inform the sitter immediately.

9. Hour cards will be paid to the sitter at the end of the sit.
10. Try to avoid cancellations. Call the sitter or gadder as soon as you know that you cannot keep the arranged agreement. The gadder is responsible for finding a replacement sitter.
11. See HOURS Section for "no-show" policy.

VI. Social Functions

1. Social functions not only are fun for the participants, they are also the only way new members can become known, and consequently used as sitters. Our co-op can survive only if we support new members by getting to know them and asking them to sit for us.
2. Members are encouraged to attend all social functions.
3. Scheduled parent/child events might include:
   * Park days—scheduled twice monthly at a day and time which is convenient for a majority of members.
      * Valentine Celebration
      * Easter Egg Hunt
      * Halloween Costume Party
      * Christmas Breakfast
      * Puppet Show
      * Your imagination
4. Scheduled adult events might include:
   * Moms' Night Out—held monthly on a day and time and at a restaurant to be decided at the monthly meetings.
      * Christmas Cookie Exchange
      * Clothing Exchange
      * Book Exchange
      * Your imagination

5. These and other events will be arranged at each quarterly meeting, and volunteers will be asked to coordinate each event. All members are asked to participate in volunteer duties, as this will keep our co-op alive, well, and fun for all.

6. All members are encouraged to donate photos of co-op events for the Co-op Photo Album, which is maintained by the Vice-President.

7. Prospective members and other guests are welcome to attend the park and pool days.

8. Members may invite guests to participate in the Moms' Night Out evenings.

9. The planning committee for each special holiday event will determine whether guests and/or prospective members may participate in the event.

THESE RULES AND REGULATIONS ARE SUBJECT TO CHANGE ACCORDING TO THE NEEDS OF THE CO-OP.

HOME VISIT REPORT

Prospective Member: _____ Date _____

Persons Conducting Home Visit: _____

Prospective Member Status: Circle one upon completion of Home Visit

ACCEPTED　　　**CONDITIONALLY ACCEPTED**　　　**REJECTED**

****

	COMPLIANCE	CONDITIONAL	NON-COMPLIANCE	NOTES

OUTSIDE

Perimeter completely fenced......Y.. N

Fence at least 4' high.............. Y.. N

Self-latching gate...................... Y.. N

Swimming pool.......................... N....................................Y (note on roster)

Spa/Hot tub............................... N....................................Y (note on roster)

Does spa have childproof
　　　cover?......................... Y.. N

Lake, stream, other body
　　　of water........................ N.. Y (note on roster)

Is water separated from yard
　　　by 4' fence?................ Y.. N

Is the gate LOCKED?................Y.. N

Is there direct access to the
water hazard from the house?... N....................................Y　(member must advise gadder & secure lock when sitting)

INSIDE

Any firearms must be key-locked with
　　　secure key location....... N....................................Y (member must advise gadder)
Unlocked/unsecured firearms.... N.. Y

Working smoke detector............ Y.. N

| | COMPLIANCE | CONDITIONAL | NON-COMPLIANCE | NOTES |

TODDLER-PROOF DESIGNATION

Does prospective member want
to comply with toddler-proof
requirements?........................... Y........................ N (will be noted on roster)
Are any of the following in an unlocked
location below 4.5':

   Medicines............................. N... Y *

   Cleaning Products................. N... Y *

   Other Poisons....................... N... Y *

   Poisons in garage................. N........................Y (garage door must be locked)

Any step-up areas to access
   poisons.................................... N........................Y (block access during sit)

Do stairs have
   an approved safety gate?........ Y........................N (must advise gadder)

* This is non-compliance <u>only</u> if member requests "toddler-proof" designation.

GENERAL

Reviewed Rules and
   Regulations............................. Y... N

Gave Emergency Authorization
   Card and explained usage........ Y... N

NOTE: A single item in the non-compliance column will cause rejection unless it is corrected to the satisfaction of the officers.

****

CONDITIONAL ACCEPTANCE:

The following must be corrected before membership into the co-op will be approved:

_____

_____

_____

_____

CO-OP EMERGENCY AUTHORIZATION CARD

Child's Name	Birthdate	Blood Type	Medical Info. (allergies, etc.)
_____	_____	_____	_____
_____	_____	_____	_____
_____	_____	_____	_____
_____	_____	_____	_____

EMERGENCY CONTACT INFORMATION

Name	Address	Phone

Husband:

_____   _____   _____

Friend:

_____   _____   _____

Doctor:

_____   _____   _____

Dentist:

_____   _____   _____

Insurance Information:

Company Name: _____   Phone #: _____

Insurance Policy Number: _____

This notarized authorization card gives my permission to treat my child. I acknowledge full responsibility for all services provided to my child in the event emergency care is needed.

_____ _____   _____ _____

Signature of Co-op Member   Date   Signature of Notary Public   Date

MOTHER'S PROFILE

Name _____ Phone _____

Address _____

Spouse's name _____ How long married? _____

Are you a full-time, stay-at-home mother?   Yes   No

If employed, please describe:_____

_____

List hobbies and special interests: _____

_____

_____

Five favorite activities you enjoy doing with your children:

_____   _____

_____   _____

_____

Favorite book: _____ Favorite movie: _____

Favorite food: _____ Favorite relaxation: _____

Briefly describe your philosophy of child-rearing:_____

_____

_____

Briefly describe your approach to child discipline: _____

_____

Why did you join the co-op? _____

_____

_____

Red Mountain Ranch
Mothers' Co-op

1234 N. Mountain Circle
Red Mountain, AZ 85215
(123) 123-1234

Contact: Cindi Lester
(123) 123-1234

For Immediate Release

BABYSITTING CO-OP NOW FORMING

Mesa, AZ -- A babysitting co-op is now being organized at
Red Mountain Ranch here in Mesa. All mothers with children
under the age of seven are invited to join. The organization,
called The Red Mountain Mothers' Co-op, will hold its
organizational meeting on May 24, 1994, at 7:00 PM, at the Red
Mountain Clubhouse.

"The co-op is a great opportunity for mothers to meet and
support each other in the task of parenting," says Cindi Lester,
the co-op's founder. "It's especially helpful for moms who are

new in the neighborhood." Lester said that the co-op will operate on a coupon system, so that no money is exchanged for babysitting services. The co-op will also host a variety of social activities for children, mothers, and the whole family. Annual dues are $20.00.

If you would like more information, please call 123-1234.

- END -

Sample press release - send after special event

Red Mountain Ranch
Mothers' Co-op

1234 N. Mountain Circle
Red Mountain, AZ 85215
(123) 123-1234

Contact: Anita Wingfield
(123) 123-1234

For Immediate Release

CO-OP EASTER PARTY FUN-FOR-ALL

Mesa, AZ -- The Red Mountain Mothers' Co-op had a great turnout for our first annual Easter Egg Hunt, held on Saturday, March 26, at the Red Mountain Park. We had 19 children participate in the fun and games.

If you are not yet familiar with the group, it is a babysitting co-op and family social club. There are nineteen member families. The group started in November 1993.

Our next quarterly meeting will be held on Tuesday, May 24 at 7:00 PM. If you would like to attend the meeting or want more information, contact Anita Wingfield at 123-1234.

- END -

Red Mountain Ranch

BABYSITTING CO-OP
<u>NOW FORMING</u>

Would you like to:

- Meet other mothers with young children.
- Exchange FREE babysitting services.
- Enjoy fun activities for your whole family.
- Have a playgroup where your child can socialize with other neighborhood children her/his own age.
- You can enjoy all this and more with the Red Mountain Ranch Mothers' Co-op.

Plan to attend our first meeting:

DATE:	Monday, April 27
TIME:	7:00 PM
LOCATION:	Red Mountain Clubhouse

For more information, call Cindi at 123-1234.

Sample business card

Red Mountain Co-op

A babysitting exchange service and family social group

We invite you to join us!

1234 N. Mountain   Mesa, Arizona 85215   (123) 123-1234

Red Mountain Ranch
Co-op News

February 1994

President: Cindi Lester 123-1234

Vice President: Anita Wingfield 123-1234

QUARTERLY MEETING NOTES

Our February meeting had a great turnout and we thank Julie for hosting the meeting at her home. Also, thanks to Sue and Joan for providing the yummy desserts and beverages.

We started the meeting by discussing the activities in December and January of last quarter and thanked Anita for hosting the wonderful Cookie Exchange. A big thanks went to Gina for all her volunteer work on laminating the half-hour cards. When you see her, say thanks again. It was a lot of work and it cut down our co-op expenses tremendously.

Our TREASURY REPORT stands at $43.00 out-of-pocket expenses and a collection of $28.00 from our last quarterly meeting. So have a negative balance of $15.00. It is normal to take about nine months before we get a positive figure in our books. Naturally, with a negative balance we will have to depend for a while on everyone pitching in for parties with goodies, etc., until we have a large enough fund.

We also discussed what the dues cover. They include the paperwork involved in running the co-op, such as copying of newsletters, roster sheets, half-hour cards (which are printed on card stock), envelopes, and information packets, etc. Excess monies can be used for our social events.

We added a new addendum to our Rules and Regulations of the co-op about associate membership. All members should attach the addendum to the back of their copy and cross out the old section on associate membership.

Our new Vice President is Clare Cooklin. Thank you, Clare, for volunteering your time.

GENERAL ANNOUNCEMENTS

Congratulations to our newest members! Dorrie McKee has two older children, ages twelve and thirteen, an eighteen-month-old boy, and a baby on the way. A new Associate member, Ann Klug, is the mother of two girls, ages three years and eleven months. Ann works full time but wants to be involved with our **Moms' Night Out** and other social events.

A new updated roster will be delivered with this newsletter. There are a couple of co-op members listed who are awaiting a home visit. Anyone who needs to schedule a home visit should contact the president or vice president. When your visit is completed, you will receive your half-hour cards and be listed on the co-op roster.

Members who were unable to attend the meeting should turn in your $4.00 dues and half-hour card to Anita or Clare as soon as possible. We will continue to publicize our co-op in the local newspaper. If you know of anyone who may be interested in joining, please invite them to any of the social events. Or, they may contact an officer to receive an information packet.

UPCOMING EVENTS

We have some fun social activities planned for the next three months. We hope to see everyone at as many functions as possible. Active participation will help us all get to know each other and our children.

- Wednesday, February 23, 3:00 PM - **Park Day at Red Rock Park**
- Wednesday, March 9, **Park Day at Falcon Field Park** at 11:00. Bring a sack lunch.
- Tuesday, March 15, 6:30 PM - **Moms' Night Out at Vito's Restaurant.** Dorrie McKee will be hosting and we will meet at her home at 6:30. Please RSVP to Dorrie. If you need to meet everyone at the restaurant, call Dorrie for directions.
- Thursday, March 24, 3:00 PM - **Park Day at Red Rock Park**
- Saturday, March 26, 10:30 AM - **Easter Party at Red Rock Park** starting at 10:30. This event is being held on a Saturday to encourage the whole family to come. We are hoping to plan a family event once per quarter. The committee will be planning an egg hunt and games. You may be hearing from a committee member to see if you can donate goodies and supplies. Or better, if you know you are coming, RSVP to a committee member and offer to help!
- Wednesday, April 13, 3:00 PM - **Park Day at Gene Autry Park**. If you need directions, call Sue.
- Saturday, April 16, 8:00 AM - **Shopping Day at the Outlet Centers** on I-10. If you've always wanted to go to these outlet stores,

and can convince your husband to watch the kids all day Saturday, sign up! Anita will be hosting this trip from her home. We will carpool from there. Don't worry. We aren't leaving the dads entirely out. We plan to have them take the kids to Red Rock Park at 11:00 AM. With sack lunches. That way, all our spouses can meet together and grumble.

- Tuesday, April 26, 11:00 AM - Tikes World and Play Center. We are meeting there. If you need directions, call Anita.
- Thursday, May 12, 11:00 AM - Fire Station Tour. We will meet at Dorrie's house and carpool over to the station together.
- Wednesday, May 18, 6:00 PM - Tuck the kids in early, because it's Moms' Night Out at The Improv. Kandace will be hosting. Call her for more details about this fun event!
- Tuesday, May 24, 9:30 AM - Pool Day at the Swim Club. Please RSVP to Lynne. If you are not a member, she will hook you up with someone who is and you can go as their guest.
- Tuesday, May 24, 7:00 PM - Quarterly Meeting will be held at the home of Ann Klug. Everyone is expected to attend!

Red
Mountain Ranch

Co-op

One Half Hour

RESOURCES

Following is a list of resources available to mothers who want to discover how to better support one another in the task of mothering:

ORGANIZATIONS

FAMILY RESOURCE COALITION
200 S. Michigan Avenue
Suite 1520
Chicago, IL 60604
(312) 341–0900

The coalition provides a vast amount of information on how to start or find parents' groups. By calling or writing, you can get a list of the existing groups in your area as well as a packet of information on how to start a group. The coalition recommends first checking the phone book under Family, Child, or Children for agencies that provide services for families. The early childhood education department of a local college might be able to tell you where to find parent education programs and support groups. Hospitals are another source of parent education/support programs. Although hospital classes may be geared primarily toward parents of newborns, such classes may be a means to start meeting other mothers.

Local churches, the YMCA, the YWCA, and the local chapter of the Childbirth and Parent Education Association also may provide local support activities or suggestions for finding them.

As a national clearinghouse, it lists more than 1,000 parent-support organizations. It supplies information for parents who wish to join an existing organization in their community or who want to begin their own.

FEMALE
(Formerly Employed Mothers At the Leading Edge)
P.O. Box 31
Elmhurst, IL 60126
(708) 941–3553

This national non-profit organization has a network of 70 local support groups for at-home mothers. The annual membership fee of $20 includes a subscription to the monthly newsletter. Local chapter start-up materials and ongoing assistance are provided. If you are interested in joining a chapter or starting one yourself, send a business-sized SASE.

GROWING FAMILIES INTERNATIONAL
9257 Eton Ave.
Chatsworth, CA 91311
(818) 772–6264

Programs include an eighteen-week parenting class, books, audio and video cassettes, a radio show, childbirth educators, a newsletter, and Contact Moms. Contact Moms is a phone line, staffed by volunteers, with an experienced mother on duty during weekdays to help you with infant or toddler questions. As a prerequisite for using the line, you must first have completed the course "Preparation for Parenting."

MOMS CLUB
814 Moffat Circle
Simi Valley, CA 93065
(805) 526–2725

The MOMS (Moms Offering Moms Support) Club, with over 160 chapters nationwide, provides information on how to start and manage a support group for at-home mothers in your area. Individual groups typically offer monthly meetings with speakers, playgroups, community service projects, instructional programs, baby-sitting co-ops, and other activities that reflect members' interests. Groups are non-denominational.

A distinction of the MOMS Club is that it is exclusively for stay-at-home moms. All events and meetings are scheduled during the day, and mothers are encouraged to keep their children with them (rather than having a separate children's program).

Anyone interested in starting a local group receives a very comprehensive start-up manual that provides detailed instructions on getting the group underway. In addition, you also will receive support from local and national representatives—not only during the start-up phase but throughout your involvement with the MOMS Club.

MOPS INTERNATIONAL
1311 South Clarkson St.
Denver, CO 80210
(303) 733-5353

MOPS (Mothers of Preschoolers) is a program designed for mothers with children under school age, infant through Kindergarten. The women are all ages and backgrounds but share the same desire—to be the best mother they can be. The goal of MOPS is to nurture all mothers of preschoolers (both stay-at-home and employed moms) to reach out with encouragement, evangelism, and effective leadership opportunities. MOPS offers a haven for frazzled nerves; an encouraging, accepting atmosphere where a mom finds out she's not alone; a quality children's program, MOPPETS, where her little ones are loved and encouraged; a relaxed atmosphere of caring, sharing, and fun; and a safe place to explore Christ's alternative to life's situations.

An experienced mother shares, based on her own experience and wisdom, about practical, meaningful ways to fulfill the varied roles of women today. Following the teaching time, the mothers break into smaller groups to discuss the topics more personally. The intimate, safe, accepting atmosphere of these groups, led by the mothers themselves, allows women to express their feelings on motherhood and marriage. They find out that they are not alone, that what they are doing does make a difference, and lifelong friendships are made.

As MOPS, women enjoy a time of crafts and creative activities. Each woman feels a sense of accomplishment, being able to bring home a completed craft, something there would probably not be the time or energy to attempt at home. Since its founding in 1973, MOPS International has grown to include more than 850 groups in the United States, Canada, and eight other countries.

MOTHERING SEMINARS, INC.
P.O. Box 712
Columbia, MD 21045
(301) 381–5195

This national non-profit organization is for parents of children from birth to three. You can bring your baby to a five-week seminar (held in homes, hospitals, or community centers) to meet other parents and to share laughter and tears and gather information. Topics include: Coping with Change; Family Relationships; Development and Stimulation; Health, Safety, and Nutrition; and Re-establishing Intimacy as a Couple. There is a nominal fee. Write for a free listing of area seminars (twenty-five branches nationwide). Send $2.00 for a training packet if you are interested in becoming a consultant to provide these seminars for other parents.

MOTHERS AT HOME
8310-A Old Courthouse Rd.
Vienna, VA 22182
(703) 827–5903

In 1984, Mothers at Home was founded as a non-profit organization devoted to the support of mothers who choose (or would like to choose) to be at home to nurture their families. Its goals are to help mothers at home realize they have made a great choice, to help mothers excel at a job for which no one feels fully prepared, and to correct society's many misconceptions about mothering.

They have published several books and offer a monthly journal called *Welcome Home*. It supports stay-at-home mothers by helping them speak with one another, thus reflecting the varied talents and unique perspectives of many different women at home.

The group also serves as a public policy advocate, making the needs of at-home moms known to government officials, the media, and others. *Welcome Home* includes such public policy information and analysis. A one-year subscription is $15.00; sample copies are available for $2.00.

An Opportunity for Your Local Women's Group

If your organization is looking for an experienced, dynamic communicator to energize an upcoming event, why not consider inviting the author? Her insightful messages and down-to-earth style are winning audiences everywhere. Donna says she is living proof that God has a sense of humor, and she always delivers an upbeat, hopeful message.

Donna has been a guest on more than 100 radio and TV programs, including the Christian Broadcasting Network, Focus on the Family, Parent Talk, National Public Radio, and Money Matters with Larry Burkett. As a conference speaker, she has addressed thousands nationwide, even speaking at the CIA. Donna is a home-based businesswoman and a home schooling mom who makes her home in Mesa, Arizona.

Some of her most popular topics include, "Overcoming the Lone Ranger Syndrome," "A Vessel God Can Use," "Becoming Who You Ought to Be," and "Earning Money at Home." If you would like Donna to lead a seminar or retreat for your group, feel free to contact her through:

> InterAct Christian Speakers Bureau
> A Division of Wolgemuth & Hyatt
> 8012 Brooks Chapel Road
> Suite 243
> Brentwood, TN 37027
> 1–800–370–9932